OF COURSE YOU'RE ANXIOUS

HEALTHY WAYS TO DEAL WITH WORRY, FEAR & STRESS IN RECOVERY

GAYLE ROSELLINI & MARK WORDEN
AUTHORS OF OF COURSE YOU'RE ANGRY

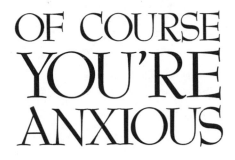

OF COURSE
YOU'RE
ANXIOUS

Also by Gayle Rosellini and Mark Worden

Of Course You're Angry

Here Comes the Sun:
Finding Your Way Out of Depression

Strong Choices, Weak Choices:
The Challenge of Change in Recovery

OF COURSE YOU'RE ANXIOUS

Healthy Ways to Deal with Worry, Fear, and Stress in Recovery

GAYLE ROSELLINI & MARK WORDEN

HarperSanFrancisco
A Division of HarperCollins*Publishers*

FIRST HARPERCOLLINS EDITION PUBLISHED IN 1991.

Library of Congress Cataloging-in-Publication Data

Rosellini, Gayle.
  Of course you're anxious : healthy ways to deal with worry, fear, and stress in recovery / Gayle Rosellini and Mark Worden. — 1st HarperCollins ed.
      p.   cm.
  "A Hazelden book."
  Includes bibliographical references.
  ISBN 0–06–255355–0
  1. Alcoholics—Rehabilitation.   2. Anxiety.   3. Stress (Psychology)   I. Worden, Mark.   II. Title.
  HV5276.R67   1991
  362.29′2—dc20   90–55299
                                                          CIP

---

91   92   93   94   95   FAIR   10   9   8   7   6   5   4   3   2   1

This edition is printed on acid-free paper that meets the American National Standards Institute Z39.48 Standard.

For Gail Pickle

CONTENTS

He has not learned the lesson of life
who does not every day surmount a fear.

— Ralph Waldo Emerson

Acknowledgments

We would like to acknowledge the beneficial influence of Alta Crawford and the usual suspects: Lynn Rosellini, John Blix, Lenore and William Horden, and Patrice Morrison. Dr. Steven K. Worden at the University of Arkansas (Fayetteville) gave us hours of entertainment with his risible accounts of sociological theory. And Carol Wikstrom has, with her customary good humor, provided us with many useful diversions.

Susinski and our good friend and neighbor, Doris Steinhauer, once again deserve special mention.

As always, we appreciate the encouragement and support of the hardworking Hazelden crew, including Pat Benson and our editors at Hazelden — Sid Farrar and Jeff Petersen.

Ducks and dachshunds and the nightly visits of the neighborhood skunk, Pepe Le Peu, added to the meaning of life during the writing of this book — as did the summer nights spent camping in our backyard Wenzel tent.

We gratefully acknowledge the following for permission to quote from the materials listed:

Psychology Today, for quote by Thomas D. Borkovec, "What's the Use of Worrying?" *Psychology Today*, December 1985.

"Psychophysiological Aspects of Caffeine Consumption." Reprinted with permission of author and publisher from: Murray, J. B. "Psychophysiological Aspects of Caffeine Consumption." *Psychological Reports*, 1988.

The Search for Serenity: Understanding and Overcoming Anxiety, Daniel A. Sugarman, Ph.D. and Lucy Freeman, New York: Macmillan Co., 1970.

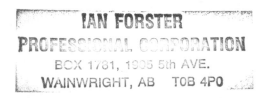

The Road Less Traveled, M. Scott Peck, M.D., New York: Simon & Schuster (Touchstone Books), 1978.

High Level Wellness: An Alternative to Doctors, Drugs, and Diseases, Donald B. Ardell, Emmaus, Pa.: Rodale Press, 1977.

"Alcohol and Nutrition: The Diseases of Chronic Alcoholism," Norman Jolliffe, in *Alcohol, Science, and Society*, New Haven, Conn.: Quarterly Journal of Studies on Alcohol, 1945.

There's Gold in Them Thar Pills: An Inquiry into the Medical-Industrial Complex, Alan Klass, Baltimore: Penguin Books, 1975. ©Alan Klass, 1975. Reproduced by permission of Penguin Books, Ltd.

Excerpt from *The Tranquilizing of America: Pill Popping and the American Way of Life* ©Richard Hughes and Robert Brewin, reprinted by permission of Harcourt Brace Jovanovich, Inc., 1979.

The A.A. Members — Medications and Other Drugs, New York: A.A. World Services, Inc., 1984.

I Want to Change, But I Don't Know How! Tom Rusk, M.D. and Randy Read, M.D., Los Angeles: Price/Stern/Sloane, 1980.

Aldous Huxley: A Biography, Sybille Bedford, New York: Alfred A. Knopf, Inc., 1973.

Actualizations: You Don't Have to Rehearse to Be Yourself, Stewart Emery, ©1977, 1978 by Stewart Emery. Used by permission of Doubleday, a Division of Bantam, Doubleday, Dell Publishing Group, Inc.

"Diagnosis and Classification of Anxiety Disorders," in *Handbook of Anxiety Disorders*, edited by Cynthia G. Last and Michel Herson, New York: Pergamon Press, 1988.

Reprinted with permission from *Alcohol* Vol. 2, Sarah M. Roelofs, "Hyperventilation, Anxiety, Craving for Alcohol: A Subacute Alcohol Withdrawal Syndrome," ©1985, Pergamon Press, Inc.

"The Abstinence Phobias: Links Between Substance Abuse and Anxiety," Sharon M. Hall, *The International Journal of the Addictions*, 19:6, ©Marcel Dekker, Inc. N.Y., 1984.

Part One

Normal Anxiety in Recovery

This is a book about anxiety — specifically about anxiety and recovery from alcoholism and other forms of chemical dependency. Anxiety is a topic of special importance for recovering people and codependents because anxiety comes with the territory.

We all get anxious, feel — to one degree or another — the momentary clutch of alarm, the heart-fluttering pang of dismay, the drawn-out lingering sense of apprehension, dread, and doom. We don't always like to admit it, but all of us experience anxiety at various times in our lives. It's important for us to know that worry, fear, shame, guilt, nerves, even panic attacks, are normal during recovery — not only for the addict, but for family members too.

CHAPTER ONE

Legitimate Distress

Anxiety — which is a form of fear — is a natural human emotion. To never feel fear is to be never fully human. But intense, uncontrolled anxiety can hurt and destroy, wreaking havoc in our relationships and eroding our self-esteem. Fear can even kill.

How many suffering people have turned to suicide as the ultimate cure for a dreadful, sick anxiety that won't end? How many spouses have been beaten, children battered and abused, loved ones murdered in a terrible storm of anxiety-fueled brutality?

More subtle than physical violence is the emotional terrorism that goes hand in hand with anxiety. When our nerves are completely raw, when our emotions are shot, a child's high-pitched giggle can drive us to distraction. We may lash out with cruel words, and we may even smash that child's natural exuberance with the hammer of our impatience.

Children are not the only victims of adult anxiety. Spouses, lovers, friends, co-workers, parents, and total strangers may suffer emotional battering because of another person's anxiety.

People will do almost anything to make this distressing emotion go away. We spend billions of dollars every year trying to control this normal human condition. We take drugs

— both legal and illegal. We turn compulsively to comforting foods, then compulsively diet to atone for our indulgence. We attend seminars, buy subliminal tapes, meditate, exercise, jog, run, bounce. We seek love, or at least a temporary feeling of intimacy, in quickie relationships.

If these methods fail us, if they end up making us feel worse instead of better, we may draw back for a while, deciding to live with our anguish. Some of us manage to get by this way. We make friends with our fears. We learn how to face our dreadful moments with our serenity and dignity intact.

But most of us aren't so lucky. When that terrible feeling of anxiety starts building up again, we seem to lose our bearings, lose all semblance of common sense. We'll do almost anything to muzzle the anxiety monster gnawing at our soul.

Too often we make futile attempts to medicate away our emotional pain with the use of alcohol and other drugs.

Necessary Anxiety & Everyday Life

Somewhere along the line, we've been sold a bill of goods about mental health. Pop psychology would have us believe that a normal, mentally healthy person is filled with happiness, love, and the joy of living at all times. It's almost as if all distressing emotions are abnormal and so are the people who experience them. One best-selling book boldly stated on the cover, "You can be happy all the time."

Nonsense!

Certainly, all of us can benefit from large portions of love and joy, but these wonderful feelings are only a part of our human capacities. If we wish to live as vital and fully aware beings, we must understand it's impossible to go through life without experiencing some loss, pain, fear, anger, and sadness. Indeed, sometimes it is *necessary* for us to suffer. Ask any woman who has borne a child if that joyful experience did not also include a good share of physical discomfort and emotional distress.

Many of us are bogged down in the *un*necessary lies, distortions, and emotional distress of chemical dependency and codependency. As a result, we haven't had the time or resources to face the *legitimate and necessary anxiety* that accompanies the emotional rebirth we call recovery.

Listen: Anxiety is a normal part of life and a necessary part of recovery. It is our willingness to suffer the emotional and physical distress anxiety brings that allows us to get beyond the darkness and personal ruin of chemical dependency and into the joy and light of positive change and growth.

Consider this: It may be our willingness to suffer *legitimate anxiety* that allows us to appreciate and experience love and happiness to the fullest.

How can this be? How can suffering improve our ability to experience positive emotions?

It works like this: Failure to examine and confront our anxious feelings will almost always inhibit recovery. Recovery, for the addict and family members alike, means acknowledging, accepting, and letting go of our problems.

This process is painful.

In *The Road Less Traveled*, psychiatrist M. Scott Peck writes:

> Problems, depending upon their nature, evoke in us frustration or grief or sadness or loneliness or guilt or regret or anger or fear or anxiety or anguish or despair. These are uncomfortable feelings, often very uncomfortable, often as painful as any kind of physical pain. Indeed, it is because of the pain that events or conflicts engender in us

that we call them problems. . . . Yet it is in
this whole process of meeting and solving
problems that life has its meaning.

According to Peck, almost all of us fear the pain caused
by confronting our problems. So we avoid looking at our
problems. We avoid the truth. We cover up and deny. This
trait, which is common to most people, is honed to a high
degree by chemically dependent people and codependents.
Indeed, one of the chief reasons we use alcohol and other
drugs is to avoid feeling the distressing emotions that are
part of dealing with our problems.

Intoxicants create enormous, life-threatening problems for
people who abuse them, but they have a great advantage for
the person who wants to avoid the normal anxiety that
accompanies everyday problem-solving. Alcohol and other
drugs block out pain immediately, RIGHT NOW!

Anxious and distressed people often use alcohol and
other drugs to avoid the *legitimate suffering* that mental
health requires. Of course, chemical dependency soon creates more pain than the original suffering. The addiction
becomes the biggest problem — the problem we must deal
with first.

Look: We're not saying that anxiety and other painful
emotions cause chemical dependency. But we are saying
that the refusal to experience normal anxiety will be a
major roadblock to recovery.

Peck says, "This tendency to avoid problems and the
emotional suffering inherent in them is the primary basis
of all human mental illness. . . . When we avoid the
legitimate suffering that results from dealing with
problems we also avoid the growth that problems demand
from us." In a sense, then, problems can be seen as challenges. When we refuse to deal with our problems — when
we avoid the challenges of legitimate suffering — we stop
growing. We become mired down, stuck. We can't mobilize

our healing resources. "And without healing," says Peck, "the human spirit begins to shrivel."

At this point we are faced with one of the great paradoxes of recovery: In order to rid ourselves of unnecessary emotional pain and anxiety, we must be willing to suffer the very pain we wish to avoid.

The only way out of anxiety is to go through it. This means we have to recognize our anxiety and deal with it directly, instead of trying to escape into some Never-Never Land of Total Bliss by using alcohol or other drugs.

Consider Judy's experience with the normal anxiety of recovery.

Judy's Story: *"I'm mad as hell, and I'm not going to take it anymore."*

Judy used all her weight to push open the big glass doors into the downtown office building where she had spent at least forty hours a week for the last seven years. A few moments later she strode into the office of the Amalgamated Insurance Company.

Her dark eyes methodically searched the familiar surroundings. The big clock on the wall behind the receptionist's desk read 8:52. The morning sun filtered through the dense jungle of philodendron foliage over by the window and spread softly across the floor at Judy's feet.

Keeping her head high and her shoulders square, she marched up to the reception desk. Her attitude was defensive, as if she expected to be thrown out.

The receptionist looked up from her coffee cup, and flashed an automatic smile. She saw Judy and the smile faltered, just for a moment, but long enough for Judy to see a momentary flash of doubt and embarrassment on the other woman's face.

"Hi," Judy said lamely. She'd tried to make her voice sound friendly and self-assured, but the one syllable came out like a strangled croak. Judy took a deep breath, hoping the lump in her throat would disappear. It didn't.

"Judy!" the receptionist said brightly, and a little too loudly. "You're back! You look wonderful, I mean, considering everything and all . . ."

"Ah . . . yes, Pam, thank you." Judy heard a door in the corridor to her left open and caught a glimpse of a face peering out before the door quietly closed. A few seconds later one of the lights on Pam's telephone lit up. Someone was making a call. Judy cleared her throat. "You were expecting me this morning, weren't you, Pam?"

"Oh. Oh, yes! Of course." Pam reached for her phone and fumbled with the receiver. "Mr. Armstrong wanted to see you at exactly nine o'clock, which is two minutes from now. I'll buzz him and you go right on down."

The path to her supervisor's office took her through the "bullpen," the bustling arena where her co-workers labored in their little cubicles. Twenty desks, but only nineteen workers behind the shoulder-high privacy screens. Judy's desk had been empty for a month, thirty-two days to be exact. Twenty-eight of those days had been spent in a chemical dependency treatment unit.

Too much alcohol, too many pills, and too much craziness had brought Judy — the bright young star of Amalgamated Insurance — crashing down with a resounding thud. She'd hidden her problem for years, hidden it from her family, from her co-workers, from herself. Then the memory black-outs had hit her. There were promises to clients she couldn't remember, and then she'd had to lie to cover her tracks, and the pressure had built up until everything exploded in a horridly embarrassing public display of drunkenness, rage, fear, and hysteria.

That last day at the office had been fueled by vodka and

little blue pills. A wild anxiety had possessed her body and mind as the fabric of her lies disintegrated around her. The worst part, the most embarrassing memory, was her unbearable grandiosity. She'd fancied herself a female version of the actor Peter Finch in the movie *Network*. She'd rampaged through the office screaming, "I'm mad as hell and I'm not going to take it anymore!"

Judy cringed at the thought. Had she really strewn client files from one end of the bullpen to the other? Had she really tried to erase the computer's memory while she ranted on about the invasion of technology into the private lives of innocent citizens? Who had she been trying to fool? Did she really think she could pass herself off as a radical champion of the oppressed masses when in reality she was trying to destroy the computer so she couldn't be uncovered as a liar and drunk and addict? The whole sorry incident would almost be funny . . . if it had happened to someone else.

Luckily, Mr. Armstrong had restrained her before she could do any real damage. Some of her co-workers had wanted to call the police, but Mr. Armstrong had taken command of the situation. Certain phrases stuck in Judy's mind: *Chemical dependency . . . employee assistance . . . treatable illness.*

Thanks to Mr. Armstrong she'd awakened in a hospital bed instead of a jail cell. But right now a jail cell seemed inviting compared to walking the gauntlet of her colleagues. The din of typewriters, telephones, and human voices filled the air. Once she had felt right at home threading her way through the labyrinth of desks, greeting her friends, solving a difficult technical problem, stopping for a moment of gossip. Now, Judy was the chief news item among the office gossipmongers.

With a deep breath Judy commanded herself to stay calm, but the fluttering in her chest refused to listen to orders. Lengthening her stride, she moved quickly through the huge room toward the back corridor and the sanctuary of Mr. Armstrong's office. A few of the people around her flashed discreet smiles. Were they greeting her or laughing at her? Not knowing the answer, and not trusting her constricted throat muscles to allow her to speak, she did nothing to encourage anyone to talk to her.

From behind the walls of one of the cubicles, Judy heard her name followed by a coarse laugh. Suddenly her anxiety turned to anger. It was as if an invisible hand had turned the faucet controlling her emotions from a slow drip of ugly anticipation to full flood. Her body was awash in adrenalin. She couldn't breathe, couldn't think. Everything was shaking, falling apart. The sweat poured off her. The pressure in her chest was choking her, and for a single terrible moment she thought she might vomit right there in front of her nineteen co-workers.

A drink. A drink! Her body, her mind, her very soul screamed for the immediate, warming comfort of alcohol. For years it had been her crutch, her lifesaver, her instant anxiety-reliever, and now, more than any other time in her life, she needed her anxiety relieved.

This was it: The moment her counselors at the treatment center had warned her about. What had they said? "At times of stress, the craving for alcohol and other drugs can become intense."

Craving. Yes, that was the right word. Judy's desire for a drink wasn't just a mere thought, a flicker of an idea. It was a sudden all-consuming physical craving, stronger than anything she could remember. Stronger than honor, stronger than love, stronger than sex.

She sucked air into her constricted lungs. The counselors had told her this might happen, but Judy had never really believed them. Yes, she had agreed, other people — weak people — might still have a desire to deal with their emotions with chemicals, but not her. Not Judy. Judy was different. She was strong. Disciplined. Sensible. Twenty-eight days in the hospital had cured her of all desire for drugs.

Sure, Judy, sure.

What had the counselors told her about this? *Think,* she ordered herself. *Remember. Everything depends on it.*

Judy forced her legs to keep moving, forced herself to breathe. She heard her counselor's voice like a soft echo over the sound of blood roaring in her ears. *Take it one day at a time, Judy. One hour at a time. One minute at a time if you need to. You can handle it, Judy. You can get through any crisis without drinking, without drugs. Easy does it. Use your coping skills. Don't be afraid of anger. Don't even be afraid of fear. They're normal emotions. You can handle it. Take a deep breath. Admit your powerlessness. Let go of your shame and pride. Put your problems in the hands of your Higher Power. Ask for guidance. And don't give in to your craving. It will pass.*

It will pass. It will pass.

Still trembling, Judy gathered up her dignity. She met the eyes of the people who were staring at her. She even managed a small smile. With her head held high, she continued on her way to her meeting with Mr. Armstrong. And as she reached his door, she resolved to say a short prayer for her co-workers. Instead of hating them, she would spend a few minutes praying for those people who laughed at her suffering.

So, Judy told herself, *I've learned something. Anxiety can make me sweat, but it doesn't have to make me drink. And I've learned something else. Those counselors knew more than I gave them credit for. I better start paying more attention to my recovery program.*

Why We Feel Anxious

Anxiety and chemical dependency go hand in hand. Those addicted to alcohol and other drugs often use the drugs to quell anxiety. But, paradoxically, the very drugs we use to medicate our distress can actually create the physical symptoms we associate with fear.

Alcohol and marijuana can trigger shaking, dizziness, and panic attacks. Amphetamines and cocaine rev up the nervous system, increase the heart rate, and cause the jittery jumpiness so common with stimulants. This overstimulation often becomes extremely unpleasant and frequently leads to dual addictions when the jangled user starts drinking alcohol or using other sedatives to calm down.

The downward spiral of addiction also intensifies problems in the areas of finances, relationships, employment, and health. Anything that threatens our survival causes anxiety, and chemical dependency is a major threat to both physical and emotional survival.

The addict's not the only one threatened — not the only one in emotional turmoil. The spouse and children of an addict carry a heavy burden of fear and uncertainty too.

Notice this: All these experiences are a *normal* consequence of chemical dependency.

Unfortunately, getting sober and straight doesn't make all that anxiety magically disappear.

Leona, a thirty-five-year-old beautician, illustrates this point: "I was on a run for about five years — heavy into alcohol and whatever chemicals I could get my hands on. The only time I was anxious was when I couldn't get high. Now it seems like I'm nervous and on edge all the time. It's an irony because when you get drug-free, your life is supposed to get easy. At least that's the theory. What happens, though, is that there are just as many hassles and just as much weirdness to deal with as before. My teenage daughter isn't doing well in school. She's real hostile and running with a bad crowd. And my mother! That's a soap opera in itself."

Leona's situation is far from rare. Chemical dependency does create soap opera lives, and even after sobriety we may find ourselves all tangled up with hostile kids and critical parents, along with many other problems. As Leona said, we still have a lot of hassles and weirdness to deal with.

The Family Soap Opera

Oddly, when the chemically dependent person gets sober and straight, family members may feel *more* anxiety instead of less. You see, when the addict is running amuck, family members have a specific problem they can blame for their feelings of distress. They can blame the booze, the drugs, the addiction.

We can hate the drugs, we can detest the addiction, and somehow still manage to love the addict. Take away the alcohol and other drug use and what do we have left? All that anxiety and nothing to blame it on.

We know that once the addict gets straight or the alcoholic gets sober, we're supposed to feel relieved and happy. But it doesn't always work that way.

Distrust lingers, nagging doubts gnaw the edges of our serenity, old wounds still hurt. We end up feeling confused and guilty.

Weren't all the simply awful family problems supposed to stop once Dad got sober?

Well, he's sober now! But the house is still filled with tension. He doesn't kick in the door and break the dishes anymore. He doesn't launch into drunken tirades like he used to. He doesn't stay out all night and leave us wakeful and terrified that the phone might ring, with a gentle official voice regretfully informing us that Dad was in a fatal accident at 2:00 A.M.

So it is better. There's a small sense of trust developing, slowly, almost as if we're cordial strangers. But there's tension in the air, tension mixed with the memories of all yesterday's pain.

You see, when we quit using alcohol or other drugs, there isn't much of an *immediate* change in the family dynamics. The situation — and the anxiety — in the family is still far from normal, far from healthy. Old habits of fear linger on.

We're supposed to be happy now, but the pain and anxiety don't magically disappear. We still have work to do.

Of course, before we decide to undertake the necessary work of recovery, we have to determine if there's a payoff. What people want to know — but often are afraid to ask — is this: *If I learn to face my bad feelings and if I put in the effort recovery requires, will my life be changed for the better?*

The answer is a resounding YES.

We're ready for recovery if we want

- to love and be loved by our family.
- to like ourselves.
- to reduce *much* of our nervousness.
- to enjoy sex more fully.
- to become more healthy physically and mentally.
- to enjoy work more.
- to have more caring friendships.
- to be less depressed.
- to learn to forgive those who have injured us and to earn forgiveness for our own mistakes.

The Anxiety Inventory

Since this book is for people who want to learn to deal more effectively with their anxious feelings, it's important to find out if anxiety is interfering with your recovery.

Just how anxious are you? What exactly are you anxious about?

Take a few minutes to fill out the anxiety inventory on the next page.

If you answered "true" to ten or more of the statements, clearly anxiety plays a big role in your life — an almost overwhelming role. It's time for a change.

If you answered "true" to five statements, you are about average in your feelings of anxiety, but learning some anxiety management techniques can make you a happier person.

If you answered "true" to even one of the last four statements (numbers fifteen to eighteen), then your anxiety has reached a danger level.

Read on to learn effective ways of coping with these distressing and dangerous feelings.

Taking Your Anxiety Inventory

To learn whether anxiety is interfering with your recovery, answer "true" or "false" to the following statements. Please, be fearless and searchingly honest: Fourth Step honest.

_____ 1. I feel a sense of impending doom.

_____ 2. I get tense and anxious when I think of the bad things people did to me in the past.

_____ 3. Waiting in line or waiting for other people makes me nervous and upset.

_____ 4. I'm jumpy and easily startled.

_____ 5. I often find myself snapping at the people who are closest to me.

_____ 6. I often lie awake at night and worry about things that upset me during the day.

_____ 7. When someone says or does something that upsets me, I don't usually say anything at the time, but later I feel nervous and distressed.

_____ 8. I'm afraid of losing control of my emotions.

_____ 9. If I get really upset about something, I have a tendency to feel sick later, either with a weak spell, headache, upset stomach, or diarrhea.

_____ 10. I worry a lot about being abandoned or betrayed.

_____ 11. When things don't go my way, I get nervous.

_____ 12. I am apt to take rejection so badly that I'm afraid to approach others for anything.

_____ 13. I've had trouble on the job because of panic attacks, overwhelming fear, nervousness, and anxiety.

_____ 14. When I'm worried and upset, I often blurt out things I later regret saying.

_____ 15. When I get worried, anxious, or apprehensive, I comfort myself with alcohol, other drugs, sex, or food binges.

_____ 16. Sometimes I feel so hurt and isolated I feel like committing suicide.

_____ 17. Sometimes my nerves are so ragged I'm afraid I might physically hurt someone who upsets me.

_____ 18. I'm an extremely anxious person, and I know I need help learning to control my fears and feelings of anxiety.

CHAPTER TWO

The Recovery Effort

For most of us, the crux of our anxiety recovery plan — our plan to acknowledge, accept, and cope with our fearful and anxious feelings — is that old standby, *knowledge.* Keep this in mind: Insight, motivation, and behavior change rely on knowledge.

Amazingly, few people possess even a rudimentary understanding of basic human emotions. Most of us go around all our lives never knowing what constitutes normal or abnormal emotional responses.

Consider these five basic emotions:

- Love
- Joy
- Anger
- Fear
- Sadness

These emotions are basic because all human beings (at least those born without major neurological damage) come into the world with the inborn capacity to experience these feelings. Our family, community, and culture teach us how to express these emotions, but we have an inborn capacity to experience love, joy, anger, fear, and sadness.

All these emotions, the pleasant and the unpleasant, are

a normal part of the human condition, and they contribute to our health and survival. Anxiety, then, which is a variation of fear, is part of our birthright. It may, indeed, be our first emotion as we are wrenched from the fluid warmth of the womb and plunged into a harsh world of intense lights and sounds. The world of the newborn infant has been described as a booming, buzzing confusion. For most of us that confusion diminishes as we grow older and learn how to cope with life.

But we will never be totally free from fear as long as our nervous system is functioning normally.

Nor should we be. Fear is an important defense, an emotion that protects us from known threats and menaces and from unknown dangers. For example, a good dose of realistic fear can help prevent us from relapsing. If we're normal, the idea of falling back into the trap of active addiction will scare us silly. If it doesn't, staying straight will be harder for us than it needs to be.

Total serenity, a life without fear and anxiety, is not a realistic goal. Total serenity would probably make us complacent and stupid. It might even lead us to relapse.

Though we might not become totally serene, we can become happier than we are now. To do that, we have to learn how to make positive changes in ourselves wherever we can. We also have to learn to accept the fact that some things can't be changed.

The Serenity Prayer expresses our situation well:

---

*God grant me the serenity
To accept the things I cannot change,
The courage to change the things I can,
And the wisdom to know the difference.*

The hard part is learning to see the difference between the things we can change and the things we can't change — learning to make a distinction between the *unchangeables* and the *changeables*.

Some Unchangeables

- We can't change anybody but ourselves.
- We can't change the past.
- We can't always get our own way.
- We can't always make people do what we want them to do.

Some Changeables

- We can change ourselves.
- We can change our future.
- We can change the way we feel when we don't get our own way.
- We can change the way we react when people don't do what we want them to do.

The Recovery Effort

The major goal of recovery from chemical dependency is becoming drug-free. Sobriety is both the beginning and the end of recovery for alcoholics and other addicts. But in the middle we find a vast area of growth and change where we can discover just how to be emotionally healthy and happy.

Now, we can stop our recovery effort after we become drug-free and call ourselves recovered. People who stop here have made a vast improvement in their lives. But what

The Power of Small, Strong Choices*

Every day you are faced with dozens of decisions, small and large, which become the stepping-stones to serenity. If your life is a mess, it's very likely that you're hurting yourself with a series of unwise decisions and poor choices. Is it possible that you are making it hard for yourself through a series of weak choices?

We have a tendency to blame our problems on other people or bad luck or forces outside our control. The real truth is that we can control a great deal of what happens to us — not everything, but enough to make a significant difference in our level of happiness.

Get this clear: You already possess everything you need for happiness, whether you know it or not. Furthermore, you have within you all the strength and sense you will ever need to overcome every obstacle life throws your way. What you need to do now is learn how to use what you already have.

To be happy, it is essential to use our power in two ways:

- We must use our inner strength and common sense to withstand the disappointment, pain, and grief we will inevitably experience in this life.
- We must use our inner strength and common sense to forge ahead in the creation of the kind of life we really want.

When you believe deep in your mind that you have the capacity, courage, and strength to take control of your life, you won't feel so nervous or tense or frightened when a new problem hits you. You will have within you the makings of serenity.

The key to achieving serenity is choice. Make no mistake, serenity is a choice. It's a choice we make step by step through a series of daily decisions. When added together, these choices — these small daily decisions — yield happiness and a sense of well-being.

*Adapted from *Strong Choices, Weak Choices*, Gayle Rosellini and Mark Worden, Hazelden Educational Materials, 1988.

about the codependent person who has never abused chemicals? And what about the sober addict who wants to keep growing?

For those of us who want to strive toward emotional health, recovery is not a goal we attain once and for all time, like a high school diploma. Once we get our diploma, we've got it. No one can take it away.

But recovery is different. It's slippery and abstract. We can feel it, but we can't put it in a frame and hang it on the wall. We can't put it away in the closet and bring it out again when we need it.

In some ways, recovery is like a magnificent oak tree. It starts as a little acorn. In a fertile environment, that acorn grows, fast at first, developing bark and limbs and leaves, so even though it may be young, within the first year it's definitely got the makings of something grand. As time passes, the seedling develops into a mature tree. But anywhere along the line, the tree can be killed — by neglect, by a storm, by deliberate sabotage.

In recovery, we have the opportunity to build upon each day of sobriety and grow to become a healthy person. But like a living tree, recovery can be killed by neglect, a stormy environment, or by sabotage. Luckily, most human beings have an advantage over plants. We can actively examine and participate in the process of our healthy growth.

And that process takes *effort*. It takes understanding and a willingness to examine the unexamined life. It takes determination to make strong choices and to make healing changes in our lives. (See box, page 20.)

Learning to deal effectively with anxiety is part of the recovery effort.

Now listen, because this is important: Recovery isn't just for the individual who has abused alcohol and other drugs. It's for the man or woman who now loves or who at one time loved an addict. It's for the son or daughter of an alcoholic or other addict. It's for the mother or father of a chemically dependent child. It's for all of us.

Each of us must go through our own recovery, because chemical dependency doesn't hurt just the addict. It hurts the family too.

Addicts, codependents, and adult children of addicts have special problems with anxiety, anger, guilt, and depression.

In families where alcohol and other drug abuse is a problem, the atmosphere hangs heavy with worry, distrust, apprehension, and fear. We become afraid of our emotions, angry with ourselves, and suspicious of our loved ones. Expressing our real feelings — the anger, the despair, the fear — may fill us with an overwhelming sense of guilt and dread.

Because we're afraid of our emotions, we say, "Well, the drinking has stopped, so let's put all the bad things away and forget they ever happened." We try to ignore our anxiety and fears, hoping all the time they'll go away. But they don't. They may even get worse. Then we get panicky because we're secretly thinking all these horrible thoughts about ourselves and the people we love. And that doesn't feel good.

A major goal of recovery is to understand that anxious feelings are a necessary part of healthy growth. We want to learn to deal with our anxiety without anger and guilt. Most importantly, we don't want our anxiety to hurt us or other people.

A cautionary note: This book won't help a person who continues to abuse alcohol and other drugs.

RULE #1 FOR ALCOHOLICS AND OTHER ADDICTS

Sobriety first, then emotional fine-tuning.

Normal Anxiety

Recovery for those of us who love or live with an alcoholic or other addict does *not* depend on that person's sobriety. It helps, but we can begin our own recovery even if that person continues to drink or use other drugs.

Here are three central elements in recovery:

- We can learn to take care of ourselves properly.
- We can learn to live our own lives instead of trying to control those around us who won't behave "right" (that is, the way we'd like them to behave).
- We can learn to let go of past hurts and get on with our lives.

Remember: Anxiety is a normal emotion.

Normal emotions don't have to be eliminated. Whether we admit it or not, we all sometimes feel anxious. We fret and worry. We become upset and frantic. Recovering people are no exception. If we've dulled our emotions for years, feelings of anxiety during recovery can be disturbing.

The idea that anxiety is a normal emotion — one that doesn't have to be eliminated — sounds odd to many of us. That's because we tend to be afraid of the intensity of our emotions.

People who have lived with chemical dependency don't merely have emotions, we have EMOTIONS!

Chemical dependency puts us in a bind — our emotions are so big, so intense that sometimes the only way we can deal with them is by turning them off. We become numb. But underneath the numbness, our repressed feelings gnaw away at the edges of consciousness. No matter how hard we try, we can never entirely silence our emotional selves. Nameless, unreasonable, free-floating anxiety is the noise of our hidden emotions clamorously begging for recognition.

For positive recovery to take place, we must examine our

anxiety, deal with its causes, and learn to make friends with our worst fears. We need to know there are healthy ways of coping with fear. And we need to learn that the management of anxiety can contribute a great deal to the process of recovery, making it less stressful and reducing the chance of relapse.

One thing to keep in mind: There's no "quick fix" for any problem that involves human emotions. There's no guru who's going to come along and wave a magic wand and make all our troubles and fears vanish instantly so that we'll live serenely ever after. And there's no drug that will vanquish fear and anxiety once and for all and leave us as alert, fully functioning human beings.

More than anything, we must be willing to look closely at sensitive areas of our lives, willing to learn, and willing to risk and be open to change.

It will take work.

We also must realize that we have a natural aversion to facing these problems. Why? Because it can be painful!

But, then, chemical dependency *is* painful. Yet the pain of recovery is nothing compared to the pain of addiction and codependency.

CHAPTER THREE

Normal Anxiety in Recovery

What are the normal anxieties we can expect in recovery? The first major fear we face is the fear of recovery. For many of us, addict and codependent alike, recovery is not necessarily seen as a blessing. It's more like a threat.

What's so scary about getting help for our problems? For one thing, recovery means change. It means moving into the unknown, which carries an element of anxiety for almost everyone.

For the addict, recovery means giving up chemicals that have become central to life. It means learning to redefine the concept of our self — to see ourselves as being drug-free addicts. It means learning how to live without alcohol or other drugs.

For family members, recovery means the possibility of revealing family secrets. Although no responsible treatment program or support group would blame a spouse or other family member for an addict's alcohol or drug dependency, there may be an element of self-blame in family members: "He wouldn't have started drinking so heavily if I were a better wife." Or: "She wouldn't have gotten addicted to pills if I were a better husband."

Children may also get anxious because they somehow feel responsible for the unhappiness of their parents' lives. This anxiety can persist long into adulthood. (See box, page 26.)

Learning Life's Lessons in the School of Dread*

For many children, the family is P.S. Dread.

P.S. Dread can be best described as an informal school system promoting denial, lies, promises, selfish martyrdom, grandiose fantasies, despair, and shame. Oh, love is there too. Lots of it. But love gets so mixed up with fear and anger and pride that sometimes we can't tell it apart from a sick kind of emotional dependence. We don't know exactly where we belong or if we are truly loved.

We learn more than anything that love is capricious, that human attachment is uncertain and perilous. We learn to hoard love, store it up for the hard times ahead. Love is surely not something to squander. We don't feel safe in P.S. Dread.

We don't feel safe in our families.

Perhaps poet Alexander Pope had P.S. Dread in mind when he wrote, "A family is but too often a commonwealth of malignants." Perhaps P.S. Dread prompted André Gide to utter the savage curse: "Families, I hate you!"

And perhaps it was P.S. Dread that anthropologist Ashley Montague had in mind when he called the family "an institution for the systematic production of physical and mental illness in the members."

Psychiatrist Karen Horney wrote vividly about troubled adults whose self-esteem is warped in a troubled family. Horney believed that neurosis develops when a person's striving for self-realization is thwarted by adverse circumstances.

And what circumstances can be more adverse for a child than the chaos and turbulence of alcoholic and codependent parents?

To cope with natural feelings of isolation and helplessness, the child develops strategies for decreasing anxiety, strategies that invariably lead to a growing sense of alienation from self: Neurotic pride; denial and reinterpretation of events; vindictive scheming against those who have caused pain; avoidance of risky situations, or procrastination.

The thwarted individual sacrifices the goal of self-realization in favor of the goal of reducing anxiety, of finding safety and security. We become stuck.

Dr. Horney could have been speaking directly to an adult child of an addict when she said the confused individual ends up not knowing "where he stands or 'who' he is."

*Adapted from *Taming Your Turbulent Past,* Gayle Rosellini and Mark Worden, Health Communications, 1987.

Then there's the prospect of having our lives put under the microscope by probing strangers, and wondering what those strangers might think about us. All this is pretty daunting, so, of course, we feel anxious.

Some of us fear becoming stigmatized — getting tagged with the undesirable label of *alcoholic* or *addict*. Or worse: *drunk* or *junkie*.

Although there have been great strides in getting chemical dependency recognized as a legitimate, treatable disorder, many people still consider alcoholism and other addictions to be manifestations of weakness or character defects. So we have to overcome our preconceived notions about what it means to be chemically dependent, and that can be both difficult and upsetting.

Here's how one recovering alcoholic remembers his anxieties about recovery: "Before I went into treatment and even for a year or so afterward, I was frightened by the thought of a life without booze. The idea of not drinking was totally alien to me, a threat to my existence. It was like I wasn't *me* any longer — I was an alcoholic, whatever that was. I didn't want to accept that. It meant I was different from other people. Now I always thought I was different from others, but not in *that* way. So I had to learn to accept some pretty unacceptable ideas about what kind of a character this new me was going to be."

Instead of squarely facing the "unacceptable," he gravitated to a life of avoidance. "I avoided social events, especially if I knew there was going to be alcohol available — and I think that was right for me. But I overdid it because I also avoided other gatherings. I just isolated myself."

Fear of Being Abnormal

If you fracture your leg and spend several days in the hospital, you can be fairly certain your friends and neighbors will express sympathy and concern, wishing you a speedy healing. They won't speculate about your character.

But if you spend several weeks in a treatment center, you can be certain that many of your friends won't understand what you've been going through. They may not know how to treat you when you return. They may try to get you to drink or do other drugs because, well, "just one won't hurt anything." Nobody wishes you a speedy recovery because many folks simply don't know about recovery. And those who do, know it's not speedy.

So we worry about what other people will think. We don't want to be seen as *abnormal*. We're humiliated by the suggestion that we're not really in control of our lives. And our anxiety may lead to a kind of defiant stance: "No one's going to tell me how to live my life."

Jack, forty-five, a millworker, describes his reaction to the perceived threat of treatment: "I've been afraid before, and I'm not ashamed to admit it. I did things in Vietnam that scared the holy hell out of me at the time, and still do — when I think about them. But I could understand that kind of fear. I was in a dangerous place. There was a real enemy. I was doing my best to inflict harm on people who wanted to kill me."

But Jack had never before felt the kind of dread that hit him when he finally admitted he had to do something about his drinking. "It was an ego-shattering terror. I had to admit that I'm an alcoholic. I had to get it through my head that alcohol was my enemy. Which was hard to do because I knew a lot of other guys who drank the way I did. We used to joke that we belonged to AU — Alcoholics Unanimous. But I can't joke about it anymore."

There were other fears: "I was afraid I was going to lose my family and my job. I could see everything valuable in my life just crumbling away. I knew I was screwed up. But I didn't think anyone else knew how screwed up I was. After I had some problems at work, they ran me through the employee assistance program and gave me a choice: Get treatment, or get another job. That made me angry and I blustered and filed a grievance. But deep down it scared me, pure and simple."

Jack went through a treatment program and is now in aftercare. "It helped a lot to learn what alcoholism is all about, and it helped to learn that I'm not alone — that I'm not some kind of slob. I'm not going to lie — I still have a hard time admitting that I'm an alcoholic. But I am, and I'm learning how to live with it. The really bright side is that most of the old terror, the old anxiety, has vanished."

Other Normal Anxieties in Recovery

Here are a few of the common anxieties we can expect to experience at some time during recovery. Keep in mind these are *normal anxieties*. Fortunately, these anxieties can be faced during early recovery and aftercare. Much of the joy of recovery comes in learning that we do not have to be permanently crippled by our dreadful feelings.

- *Fear of withdrawal symptoms.* Giving up alcohol and other drugs may result in acute withdrawal symptoms. An addicted person always feels some form of discomfort during withdrawal, but modern medical treatments have lessened the horrors of delirium tremens (D.T.s), and hallucinations involving pink elephants and snakes are extremely rare.

- *Fear of emotional or physical pain.* Many of us have used alcohol and other drugs to self-medicate away our distressing emotions or chronic pain problems. What we fear is not pain so much, as *feeling*. But with recovery, we find that feeling includes a lot of good things too.

- *Fear of talking in recovery meetings or group therapy or education classes.* Surveys show that public speaking scares more people than any other normal activity. This is true for non-addicts and addicts alike.

- *Fear of self-disclosure.* There are some things we fear disclosing to others because we are apprehensive about their reaction. Surprisingly, even our worst exploits hold little shock value because during active addiction and codependency we've all done our share of foolish and shameful things.

- *Fear of sober sex.* Many men and women have not had a sexual relationship without the mediation of alcohol or other drugs. Some addicts also have a history of trading sex for drugs, so sex is associated with the seamier aspects of life before recovery.

- *Fear of leaving treatment.* People who undergo treatment in an inpatient setting frequently fear the end of treatment. They dread going back to their family. Or they dread going back to their empty apartment. They dread going back to work. Or they recoil from the prospect of looking for a job, trying to find references, trying to account for lost time.

- *Fear of socializing without intoxicants.* We may feel socially awkward around other people, not knowing how to gracefully decline the offer of a drink. We may feel like oddballs, thinking that other people are commenting unfavorably on our refusal to imbibe or take drugs.

*Abstinence Phobias**

Psychologist Sharon M. Hall suggests that abstinence phobias occur in virtually all addicts:

"Once a person has become psychologically or physiologically dependent upon a substance, and consciously recognizes this dependency, anticipation of termination of drug use, or even reduction in dose, can produce anxiety."

Her model of abstinence phobias shows anxiety generated from two primary sources:

1. *Overreaction to mild withdrawal symptoms.* This overreaction may occur because

- addicts have past experiences with severe, painful withdrawal.
- addicts have inaccurate models of withdrawal based on misinformation from street lore or dramatizations.

2. *Fear of being drug-free.* This may arise from
- lack of emotional coping skills.
- lack of life-support skills and interpersonal skills — in effect, lack of social competence. Being drug-free means giving up a drug-centered life and taking on new responsibilities. It means forming drug-free relationships. It means finding and holding a job and facing the demands and everyday hassles of life.

Hall contends that abstinence phobias during the detox phase of recovery perpetuate a vicious circle, by increasing feelings of helplessness and setting the stage for further drug use. This pattern is then followed by another cycle of detox-phobia-drug use.

For many people, recovery depends on acknowledging their abstinence phobias and dealing with them directly to prevent relapse.

* Adapted from "The Abstinence Phobias: Links Between Substance Abuse and Anxiety," Sharon M. Hall, *The International Journal of the Addictions,* 1984.

- *Fear of looking bad.* Most of us possess the normal desire to look good in the eyes of other people. We fear that by admitting our lives are unmanageable, we'll look like incompetent dopes instead of heroes. If we relapse, the fear of looking bad can prolong our suffering by making us too proud or too ashamed to face our recovery group again.

Reality Rebound

Sometimes getting sober can make anxiety worse. Alcohol and other drugs blot out painful reality, at least temporarily. When we're high, we can ignore the things that frighten us. It's no wonder that for years, alcohol has been known as *liquid courage.* Alcohol and other drugs actually medicate our minds, anesthetizing the sections of our brains that register fear.

So when we sober up, when we stop artificially medicating our brains, we are suddenly faced with *reality* in living color and stereoscopic sound, smell, taste, and touch. Raw sensations come flooding in from all sides, and they can be overwhelming. We are confronted by the past, present, and future, with nothing to dull the sharp edges of awareness.

Let there be no doubt: This kind of sensory awareness can be confusing and frightening to someone who has systematically used alcohol or other drugs to dull the senses for months or years or decades.

We are also faced with the reality of our emotions. Our inner lives have been numbed for so long that we are disconcerted when we feel raw emotion once again. We may be frightened by our anger. We may be totally unprepared for grief and sadness. We may even feel like we're going crazy when we experience the normal anxieties of everyday life.

But we're not going crazy. We're simply experiencing

reality rebound. We're alive and aware and again like newborn babes, facing the booming, buzzing confusion of an unfamiliar world.

Love and joy and friendship boggle us.

In the past, we knew how to get high, but we did not know how to give and receive love.

We knew how to blot out our problems, but we did not know how to experience joy.

We knew how to be glib and charming among strangers, but we did not know the inexpressible pleasure of decent friendship.

There's another anxiety-provoking aspect to reality rebound: Facing the music. Taking responsibility for the everyday duties we've neglected because of our chemical dependency or codependency. There are bills to face. There are relationship problems that can no longer be avoided by taking a pill, going to a bar, or throwing a temper tantrum.

Recovery rebound always increases nervous tension. So it's important to remember this: *For recovering people, anxiety is the monster that can trigger relapse.*

But it's equally important to keep this in mind:

RELAPSE IS NOT INEVITABLE

We can learn ways to reduce our anxiety.

We can learn ways to keep anxiety from undermining our recovery.

We can learn to face our fears, accept ourselves and our emotions, and become open to love and joy and friendship.

CHAPTER FOUR

The Screaming Meemies

There's a strong *physical reason* why recovering people may experience more anxiety than they did in their using days. It's known that people who use alcohol and other mind-altering drugs to excess lose much of their dream sleep. Scientists don't know why people dream or even why people sleep, but research indicates that everyone dreams whether they recall it or not. More: Dreaming is essential to proper brain function.

To Sleep, But Not to Dream

When we lose normal dream sleep due to excessive alcohol or other drug use, we don't lose our *need* for dream sleep. And that creates a problem. When we get sober, our brain starts playing dream catch-up — and we dream with a disturbing intensity.

Many recovering people report that during the first months of sobriety they feared going to sleep. Every time they dozed off, they fell almost instantly into unpleasant dreams that turned into bloody, screaming nightmares. Old-timers call this phenomenon the *screaming meemies*, and it really puts the recovering person in a bind.

We need sleep to restore our strength and serenity. Our bodies need time to rest and heal.

In early recovery, however, sleep often becomes a journey into terror, a time of weird nightmares, cold sweats, muscle aches, spasms, and cramps. This situation produces several predictable problems for recovering people:

- *Fear of sleep* creates acute insomnia, which gives us more to worry about and more time to worry.
- *Lack of sleep* creates exhaustion, and when we're fatigued, our nerves are frayed.
- *Exhaustion and anxiety* spur us to seek relief, and frequently the relief that's worked best in the past is alcohol and other drugs.

So we find ourselves in a vicious circle: Use of intoxicants robs us of needed dream sleep; sobriety intensifies unpleasant dreams; nightmares create craving for intoxicants to stop dreams. We're damned if we do and damned if we don't.

But there's good news: The screaming meemies is a temporary condition. We will not feel this way forever. We are not going insane. And, yes, we will be able to sleep again, and there will again be nights filled with sweet and pleasant dreams.

We must remember that this period of disturbed sleep is a natural part of recovery. Just knowing that this unpleasant phenomenon is a normal part of sobering up can go a long way in helping us get through this distressing time without relapsing.

Craving

Make no mistake: The distress and anxiety created by disturbed sleep patterns can create a strong craving for alcohol and other drugs. The craving recovering people experience for their favorite drug has much in common with anxiety.

Like anxiety, craving comes in varied intensities. It may

be relatively mild, or it may be intense. Researcher Arnold Ludwig describes the differences between mild and strong craving: "A sense of tension, unease, irritability, restlessness, insecurity, self-disgust, vague guilt, or annoyance are all associated with mild craving."

In strong craving, Ludwig notes, the person's feelings are naturally more intense: "Distress, depression, shakiness, apprehension, jumpiness, a knot in the stomach, the fear of dying, and a feeling of sickness or of being out of control are equated with strong craving."

Ludwig points out that drinking even small amounts of alcohol can trigger craving and "the heightened response to small amounts of alcohol consumed under appropriate conditions offers strong support for the AA injunction against taking the first drink."

Other factors may whet the appetite for alcohol or serve as chemical triggers for craving. Almost any drug that provides a high may stimulate the desire to drink. Minor tranquilizers, such as Librium and Valium, or barbiturates can serve as continual reminders of the feeling of intoxication and can intensify craving.

Willard, a forty-eight-year-old motel manager, vividly recalls how his screaming meemies kept the embers of craving alive: "I actually thought I would never sleep again. I relapsed on two separate occasions because I tried to drink myself to sleep. Oh, I slept all right, but believe me, it wasn't worth it."

Willard's wife, Stephanie, talks about her confusion and anxiety during this period: "I didn't understand what was going on. I was dismayed when Willard whimpered and screamed in his sleep. I really thought a couple of times that he was going crazy. And when he fell off the wagon, I was certain he was going crazy."

But Willard didn't go crazy. "I've been sober now for two years," he says, knocking on wood and patting the Big Book. "Each time I sobered up, I had bad dreams for about three months. I don't know what it is about the third month for me — that's when I relapsed both times. But I finally got through it — one day at a time — and now I sleep like a baby. A sober baby."

Beating the Screaming Meemies

What can a recovering person do to combat the screaming meemies? A lot. We can cope in three different ways.

1. Mental Attitude

- Remember, disturbed sleep patterns are a normal part of sobering up.
- Don't worry that you're going crazy. Your nightmares may be horrible, but they are caused by your brain regaining its normal dream function, not by a kink in your personality. The nightmares will eventually stop.
- Think of insomnia as a temporary inconvenience instead of a major catastrophe. Lack of sleep may leave you feeling lousy, but it won't cause any permanent physical or emotional damage. You will sleep again.

2. Living Habits

- Get up in the morning before 9:00 A.M., no matter how unrested you are. Many insomniacs toss and turn all night, then snooze until late in the day or take short naps. These habits create nighttime restlessness.
- Exercise your body. Physical exercise can help you relax and rids the body of built-up waste products. Take a walk, do calisthenics, ride a stationary bike, do a video workout. It doesn't matter what you do, but try to move vigorously for twenty minutes a day.

- Try eating starchy foods during your evening meal such as breads, pasta, rice, potatoes, or beans. Starchy carbohydrates contain natural elements that make some people feel calm and sleepy.

3. Drug-Free Lifestyle

- Don't use coffee or other drinks with caffeine (tea, many soft drinks) after 3:00 P.M.
- No matter how sleepy you are, don't use wake-up or pep pills of any kind, legal or illegal. Over-the-counter diet pills should also be avoided because they contain stimulants.
- No matter how nervous you are, don't use nerve pills, tranquilizers, or sleeping pills of any kind, legal or illegal.
- In short, don't try to drink, smoke, snort, inject, or swallow your anxiety away.

How long does it take for the screaming meemies to pass? Some people return to normal sleep and dream patterns after a few weeks of sobriety. For most people, sleep will gradually return to normal over several months. A few people suffer nightmares and insomnia off and on for a year or more.

Who's most likely to suffer the longest? It's the cheater, the person who tries to take one little drink, one little toke, one little line, one little pill.

Cheating prolongs the agony indefinitely and inevitably leads to a full-blown relapse.

Part Two

When Anxiety Disables

We've said that anxiety during recovery is normal, but sometimes our distress goes outside the bounds of normalcy. Some of us go beyond feeling tense and nervous. We're downright irrational. When that happens, we may have what's called an anxiety disorder.

Anxiety disorders are formal, psychiatric illnesses. They create long-standing personal misery and family distress. They can even be disabling.

The bad news is that alcoholics, other addicts, adult children of addicts as well as people with codependency problems seem to be vulnerable to anxiety disorders. Now the good news: With proper treatment, most people can recover from anxiety disorders.

CHAPTER FIVE

Panic & Phobias

The immediate physical and emotional experience of normal anxiety and an anxiety disorder are pretty much the same — both feel awful. But there is a difference.

Normal anxiety is an appropriate response to any new or threatening situation. Admitting we have an addiction, checking into a treatment center, attending a recovery meeting, examining our character defects, facing job and family sober — all of these things can be pretty darn scary. Under these circumstances, it's perfectly appropriate to feel nervous and sweaty. We may be scared, but our fear is grounded in reality.

An *anxiety disorder*, on the other hand, describes inappropriate fear — fear that is both persistent and irrational. The fear that a person with an anxiety disorder feels is real, but it's not based on reality. It's distorted, exaggerated, all out of proportion to what's really happening.

ANXIETY AND FEAR ARE NORMAL EMOTIONS

Anxiety disorders are distortions of normal emotions.

We may have an anxiety disorder if

- anxiety avoidance becomes the controlling factor in our lives.
- our anxiety is unreasonable or totally out of proportion to real life threats.
- anxiety prevents us from leaving the house or dealing with other people in a normal way.
- we use bizarre thoughts, rituals, or behaviors to control our anxious feelings.
- our anxiety hangs on indefinitely with no let-up in sight.

Let's now look at some of the anxiety disorders and how they can complicate recovery.

Simple Phobias

The anxiety disorder most of us have heard about is the phobia. A phobia is a *persistent and irrational fear* of a specific object, activity, or situation. Our fear is so great that we'll go to any length to avoid the thing that scares us.

Common phobias include:

- Fear of closed spaces (claustrophobia)
- Fear of heights (acrophobia)
- Fear of tests (test anxiety)
- Fear of blood (hematophobia)
- Fear of the number 13 (triskaidekaphobia, which is generalized into superstitious behavior that leads a person to stay in bed on Friday the 13th, or which leads architects to eliminate the 13th floor from tall buildings)

Not all persistent fears can be labeled phobic. Ogden Nash wrote of a basic fear response:

> Whenever I behold an asp,
> I can't suppress a startled gasp.

Screaming at the sight of a scary object doesn't signal a full-blown phobia unless we get so busy avoiding the scary thing that it begins to interfere with our lives.

For example, one woman in a group for codependents revealed that her fear of snakes was so extreme that she refused to watch television or read books because a snake might be involved in the program or story. She couldn't take her children to toy stores because she might come face to face with a toy snake. She couldn't go grocery shopping because spaghetti and rope licorice made her think of snakes. She couldn't visit a garden shop because hoses looked like giant boa constrictors. And of course, she couldn't engage in any outdoor activities because snakes lived outside. Clearly, her fear of snakes had gone beyond the normal "startled gasp" and into the range of a mental dysfunction.

This woman had never talked to anyone about her phobic responses before. Because she was ashamed, she made all sorts of excuses, and as a result her family life was a total mess. She (and her family) had suffered for almost twenty years. But after she brought her problem out in the open and agreed to see a therapist specializing in the treatment of phobias, she rid herself of her irrational fear in a few months. This allowed her to get on with dealing with the other important issues in her life.

Special Relevance for Recovering People

Our problems don't get solved by keeping them secret. It's vital that we openly confront our fears and deal with them directly instead of avoiding everything that makes us anxious. If we don't know how to do this on our own, we must be willing to ask for professional help.

Social Phobias

Social phobias involve persistent, irrational fears of public humiliation and embarrassment. These fears are accompanied by an intense avoidance of any situation in which we may be exposed to scrutiny. A social phobia is something like shyness carried to an extreme.

Common social phobias include:

- Public speaking or performance.
- Using bathrooms where other people might hear or see you.
- Eating in public.
- Swimming in public.
- Walking in front of people, such as walking through a restaurant.
- Writing in the presence of others.
- Asking directions.
- Speaking to strangers.
- Attending social affairs.
- Dating.
- Dealing with authority.

If we have a social phobia, the prospect of public performance of any kind may generate *anticipatory anxiety*. Just thinking about speaking in front of other people may scare us out of our wits. Our anxiety level is so high, we imagine everyone will be looking at us, judging us, and finding us lacking. We feel humiliated, angry, hurt, and defiant all at the same time, and we'll do anything to avoid making public fools of ourselves. Which usually doesn't work, because no matter what we do, we end up feeling foolish. That's part of the disorder.

Special Relevance for Recovering People

A social phobia can interfere with recovery if the prospect of attending group therapy or recovery meetings produces anxiety. We can suffer conflicting emotions: We may feel terrified about being singled out for attention. But we may also fear that we might get lost in the shuffle and not be recognized as a special or important person.

This dreadful anticipation, in turn, makes us want to avoid the source of our terrible feelings — the recovery meeting or therapy group.

Social phobics usually feel embarrassed about these unreasonable fears. We know our fear is out of proportion, but it's beyond our ability to control. So we end up making all sorts of lame excuses to get out of participating in group therapy, AA, Al-Anon, or other recovery groups.

If a social phobia prevents us from fully participating in the recovery process, there are three things we must do:

1. *Stop making lame excuses.* It's vital that we face this problem squarely. We must honestly tell our addiction treatment counselors the truth about our unreasonable fears and anxieties.

2. *Start making positive changes.* We may need the help of a therapist to create a plan of change that addresses both our addiction and our social fears.

3. *Develop a buddy system.* It's often easier to attend a recovery meeting if we go with a friend who understands our problems. Even if we are afraid to speak, we can learn a lot by listening. As we become more comfortable with the group, we may find we are able to say a few words. Psychologists now have proof of an old proverb: When we do the thing we are afraid of, soon we lose our fear of it.

Agoraphobia

The word *agoraphobia* literally means "fear of the marketplace," although it is more commonly thought of as being afraid to go out into public places alone. In a nutshell, agoraphobia is *the fear of feeling caught or trapped in some place or situation from which one cannot make a speedy and graceful escape to a place of safety.*

Many agoraphobics refuse to seek treatment because they fear to venture away from home. Physical and mental symptoms can be so intense that the sufferer actually collapses when he or she attempts to perform ordinary duties and chores outside the home. Agoraphobia may be accompanied by panic attacks, and individuals also frequently suffer from depression.

Agoraphobics often insist on taking a companion, friend, or family member whenever they leave home. This can lead to damaged family relationships because young children frequently end up taking care of their disabled parent. This upside-down family dynamic puts an unfair emotional burden on the child, straining the very fabric of family life. About two-thirds of agoraphobics are women.

Special Relevance for Recovering People

A Canadian study of 511 patients admitted for chemical dependency found that about one-third of them could be diagnosed as having some sort of phobia, with agoraphobia being the most severe and pervasive form.

Agoraphobia occurs more often in people who come from families where other members of the family suffer alcoholism and depression. Some scientists think there may be a genetic link between these problems.

If a person is both chemically dependent and agoraphobic, *the chemical dependency must be treated first.* Active addiction will often subtly mask and mimic other symptoms, thus rendering all treatment attempts futile until the addict is clean and sober.

Panic Disorders

When we have recurrent panic or anxiety attacks at unpredictable times, we may be developing a panic disorder.

Please note: The terror or anxiety caused by severe physical exertion or by a life-threatening situation can be called *panic*, but it is not the same thing as a *panic disorder*. In a panic disorder, spontaneous panic attacks seem to come "out of the blue," for no apparent reason.

The checklist on page 50 describes the most common symptoms of panic, along with the basis for a diagnosis of a panic disorder.

Panic Symptoms Checklist

Here is a list of the symptoms psychiatrists look for in a panic attack. If you have felt anxiety that seems to strike without warning, check the symptoms you remember suffering.

____ Shortness of breath.

____ Irregular or rapid heartbeat: The old ticker flops around like a frantic frog in a paper sack.

____ Chest pain or discomfort: Sometimes leads people to mistakenly believe they're having a heart attack.

____ Choking or smothering sensations.

____ Dizziness or unsteady feelings: This can lead to staggering or actually falling.

____ Feelings of unreality: Suddenly feeling like you're standing apart from yourself, like you're watching yourself through the wrong end of a telescope.

____ Tingling in hands or feet.

____ Hot and cold flashes: A sudden rush of blood to the head — almost like blushing, only there's nothing to blush about — or sudden chills.

____ Cold sweat: A clammy, unpleasant perspiration that often seems to have an unusually strong odor.

____ Trembling and shaking: This shakiness is usually most apparent in the hands.

____ Faintness: On the verge of collapse.

If you identified *four* of the symptoms during one episode, you have probably experienced a panic attack. A diagnosis of panic disorder is based on

- at least *three* panic attacks within a three-week period, where there was no physical exertion or no life-threatening situation.
- at least *four* of the major symptoms of a panic attack must occur during each episode.

Special Relevance for Recovering People

Research shows that between 3 and 5 percent of the general population report suffering from occasional panic attacks. But a number of counselors who work with chemically dependent people and adult children of alcoholics indicate that many of their male clients and even more of their female clients report that at times they suffer panic attacks so severe *they think they are going to die.*

It's clearly important to understand as much as we can about the causes of panic attacks and how to prevent them during recovery.

The Hyperventilation-Anxiety Connection in Recovery

When people *overbreathe*, they may feel dizzy, out of breath, and faint. Sensations of numbness, tingling, muscle cramps, and pounding of the heart may also occur. This condition is known as *hyperventilation*. When people overbreathe, they take in too much air, and they exhale too much carbon dioxide. Lower levels of carbon dioxide stimulate more breathing, so that the person feels the need to breathe even more vigorously.

Studies done in the Netherlands indicate a strong connection between alcohol withdrawal and hyperventilation. About 30 percent of inpatient alcoholics may suffer from anxiety due to hyperventilation during periods of abstinence ranging from weeks to months.

Here are some common symptoms of hyperventilation:

Rapid heartbeat Feeling of unrest, panic
Pounding heart Shivering

Suffocating feeling	Irregular heartbeat
Pressure on chest	Tenseness
Need for air	Nausea
Fainting	Trembling hands
Headaches	Fits of crying

Tingling in feet, legs, fingers, or face
Faster and deeper breathing than normal

Symptoms of hyperventilation and anxiety are closely interwoven and appear to trigger craving for alcohol during withdrawal *up to nine months or more following treatment.* These symptoms of anxiety and craving are most severe in those who have longer drinking histories and who have the greatest duration of dependence on alcohol.

The hyperventilation-anxiety connection is often overlooked in recovery. The Netherlands research warns:

"Hyperventilation can occur without a visible increase in respiratory rate or volume and is therefore not recognized by the patient or physicians."

The Netherlands research also suggests that the "dry shakes" and the often reported panic attacks during late withdrawal may be related to hyperventilation. Fortunately, the symptoms decrease with prolonged abstinence.

This information is important to recovering people because the symptoms of hyperventilation are so disturbing we may be tempted to treat them by drinking or taking legal or illegal drugs.

Treating symptoms in this manner inevitably leads to full-blown relapse.

Preventing Hyperventilation

Hyperventilation, a form of over-breathing, creates symptoms so distressing we can feel as though we are about to die.

"I felt as though I had a boulder on my chest," says Robert, a former hyperventilator. "I was breathing as hard as I could, but I felt like I couldn't get any air into my lungs. I had my wife rush me to the hospital because I was positive I was dying. I felt numb all over, and my fingers and toes were so stiff they were practically bending backwards."

Robert wasn't dying. Although he felt awful, he wasn't even ill. "I was in the middle of an argument with my teenage son when this thing struck me. I was so angry I wanted to hit him, but I was trying to control myself. That's when I started to feel like I was smothering. Of course, I immediately thought I was having a heart attack."

At the hospital, a doctor quickly determined that Robert's heart was sound. Recognizing the symptoms of hyperventilation, the doctor explained the problem to Robert and led him through some breathing exercises.

"I didn't buy it," Robert confesses. "It seemed impossible to me that something as simple as breathing too much could make me feel like I was ready to croak. I left the hospital pretty angry."

Several days later, Robert suffered another attack. "Before rushing to the hospital," he says, "I did what the doctor had told me to do. In about five minutes I was better. In the next couple weeks I had two more attacks that I stopped as soon as they started. I was sold. I haven't had an attack since."

Doctors say the oxygen-carbon dioxide ratio can be rebalanced by breathing into a paper bag (not plastic!) during an acute attack. Awareness is vital. Hyperventilation can be totally controlled by conscious effort.

CHAPTER SIX

Obsessions, Compulsions &
Post-Traumatic Stress

Compulsions are behaviors; obsessions are thoughts. Compulsive behaviors and obsessive thoughts are recurring, persistent, irrational, uncontrollable, almost irresistible impulses. For example, a compulsive young man washed his hands until they bled; an obsessive woman made herself sick worrying that her son might choke while eating. These cases are extreme. Compulsive house-cleaners and obsessive lovers are far more common. These are people who appear to function well, but who take normal activities to an annoying and even dangerous extreme.

Obsessive-compulsive behaviors follow the distinct pattern of the vicious circle:

- Certain urges are so compelling that resisting them creates intense anxiety.
- Giving in to the urge immediately relieves the distress, even when the urge is clearly destructive, stupid, or irrational.
- The relief only lasts a short time and may be followed by shame or pangs of guilt.
- Soon more urges strike, along with more anxiety, and more stupid, self-destructive behavior.

A good example of the obsessive-compulsive vicious circle is the compulsive dieter daydreaming about hot fudge sundaes. The more she diets, the more she thinks about the rich, gooey warm chocolate and the cool, creamy ice cream. When she's supposed to be thinking about her job or family or other important things, she's thinking chocolate.

Her thinking becomes increasingly selfish, shallow, and one-dimensional. Finally she gets so edgy and obsessed with food, she gives in, bingeing on enough ice cream and hot fudge to feed Boy's Town. Later, filled with self-disgust, she compulsively diets to atone for her binge. Then she starts thinking about hot fudge sundaes. . . .

Special Relevance for Recovering People

It's particularly important for recovering people to understand the obsessive-compulsive vicious circle because our urge to drink or use other drugs resembles an obsessive-compulsive disorder. Thoughts about sneaking a drink or taking one little line of cocaine can invade our consciousness like a senseless, repugnant intruder. We may attempt to suppress or ignore these thoughts, but that doesn't make them go away.

We also tend to keep these thoughts secret because we don't want people to think we're bad or weak. We don't want others to get upset and punitive towards us because we know we're not supposed to be thinking these kinds of thoughts if we're really recovering.

So what happens to a lot of us is this: We start making plans for a secret binge. We tell ourselves that we'll check into a motel room, and we'll spend one day or maybe a weekend getting blasted — getting it out of our system. No one else will ever know about it, so no one will be hurt. This way we'll get all these urges out of our system, and we'll be able to go back to our jobs and families totally in control.

Yes! Yes! We really do think this destructive stuff! All these dangerous thoughts go on secretly in the minds of many of us while we're in treatment, attending group therapy, recovery meetings, and talking about how grateful we are for our sobriety.

Non-addicted codependents are often obsessive about food or about controlling the lives of the people around them. The subject of the obsession is different, but the process is the same.

Let there be no mistake: *This type of obsessive thinking leads directly to relapse.* And it explains why there is often at least one person who appears to be totally sincere and gung ho in treatment, but who gets wiped out within two days after leaving the treatment center.

DON'T LET THAT PERSON BE YOU.

What can you do when obsessive thoughts of alcohol and other drugs invade your mind?

1. *Don't feel like the Lone Ranger.* You are not alone in your obsessive thinking. You are not weird, or bad, or weak. But you may feel like you're the only one with this problem because nobody likes to talk about their awful thoughts, feelings, and urges. Recognize that obsessive-compulsive feelings about alcohol and other drugs are part of chemical dependency. You are experiencing a common and expected problem of recovery.

2. *Talk about it.* Honestly tell your therapist or recovery group about your thoughts. Don't be too surprised if a couple of people come down on you like a ton of bricks. They've probably had the same kinds of thoughts. Their anger and disgust are aimed as much at themselves as at you.

3. *Don't for one little minute start believing that you can drink or use drugs just once.* Recovery means being clean and sober all the time. One slip is a relapse. Don't fool yourself into thinking you can get away with cheating and still call yourself recovering.

Post-Traumatic Stress Syndrome

If something really awful happens to us, something outside the range of usual human experience, we may develop post-traumatic stress syndrome. In the public mind, this condition is usually associated with combat veterans from the Vietnam War. But victims of rape, other crimes of violence, and incest probably form the largest group of people suffering post-traumatic stress. They are also the least recognized victims, often suffering in silence for years, too ashamed to talk about the terrible things that happened to them.

While events such as bereavement, chronic illness, business losses, or marriage conflicts can cause us emotional pain, they are not considered to be the kinds of trauma that cause post-traumatic stress. In other words, having a job you hate may stress you out, but you won't develop post-traumatic stress unless something really terrible happens, such as an armed gunman attacking your office building and holding you hostage.

Some events known to trigger post-traumatic stress disorder include:

- Natural disasters (floods, earthquakes, fires)
- Man-made disasters (car and airplane crashes, bombings, torture, concentration camps)
- Civilian or military involvement in a war zone

- Medical duty in war or other disasters
- Kidnapping, criminal assault, rape
- Sexual abuse, repeated beatings, or long-term emotional torture in dysfunctional families

Not all post-traumatic stress disorders are the same. Traumas stemming from war and violent crime seem to affect people more deeply than those from natural disasters. Most victims of torture develop the disorder, but only a few car-crash victims succumb. Some people are only mildly impaired. In others, it may affect every area of life. And some people may suffer for a few months, while others experience symptoms for years, often not recognizing the relationship between their current distress and the original trauma.

Major Symptoms of Post-Traumatic Stress Disorder

- Reliving the traumatic event (in dreams, flashbacks, or recurring and intrusive memories of the event).
- Feelings of detachment and estrangement from others.
- Blunting of emotional responsiveness.
- Reduced involvement with the outside world.
- Marked decrease in ability to enjoy intimacy, tenderness, and sexuality.
- "Psychic numbing" or turning off of normal emotions.
- Distrust of the world in general.
- Increased arousal and hypervigilance, with an exaggerated startle response.
- Difficulty in concentrating.
- Insomnia, nightmares.
- Anxiety, depression, and guilt.
- Phobic avoidance of activities that arouse recollection of the trauma.
- Alcoholism and other drug abuse.

Special Relevance for Recovering People

Life in families where one or more family members are addicted is pure hell. Psychiatrist George Vaillant compared living in an alcoholic family with being an inmate in a concentration camp. And Dr. Timmen Cermak boldly states that many people from chemically dependent families suffer post-traumatic stress.

Not all of these families qualify as torture camps. But we can't deny that some do. We're not talking here about mere unpleasantness or grumpy parents. We're talking about families where battering and other forms of brutality take place — such as sexual abuse and mental torture.

Children who survive the crucible of parental terrorism may enter adulthood suffering both post-traumatic stress and chemical dependency problems. Battered spouses who work up the courage to leave their abuser may also suffer from both conditions. And so can accident victims and combat veterans.

Both chemical dependency and post-traumatic stress are serious, even life-threatening, disorders. Both need to be treated. *And under all circumstances, the chemical dependency needs to be treated first.*

It doesn't matter which problem came first, or if they came together, or if one seems worse than the other. All attempts to treat post-traumatic stress while the sufferer remains actively chemically dependent will end in failure.

Ted's Delayed Stress Syndrome

Ted enlisted in the army when he was seventeen, encouraged by his father who said, "It will make a man out of you."

"It made a grunt out of me," Ted says. "I learned how to shoot a rifle. I learned how to drink and get high."

Ted was in combat and came away shaken by the sight of wounded and dead buddies. He also came away shaken by some of the things he did to the enemy with his rifle and his knife, things that came back in nightmares long after he left Vietnam.

Like many other young men who went to other wars, Ted came home and floundered. After the life-threatening intensity of Vietnam, civilian life in the States seemed dull and meaningless. He was home, but he felt as if he were in a foreign country — not as a soldier this time, but an anonymous person with no real role in life.

He came home expecting to be recognized as an important person, and found that nobody cared. He found that many of the other young men in his community — guys he'd known in school — thought he'd been a fool for risking his life for nothing in Vietnam. Ted began drinking more and turned to other drugs with increasing eagerness. Alcohol and drugs dulled the pain and erased the humiliation. Drinking and smoking dope made him feel like a man. And when he fought in bars — as he often did — he proved he was a man. At least in his own mind. Even when he got whipped, even when he came away bloody and battered.

So Ted drank too much, smoked too much dope, and went through job after job. At times he was morose and suicidal, and at other times his temper flared unpredictably and he struck out. He fought like a madman in bars, a frenzied, desperate kind of fighting, as if he didn't care about who he hit or why. As if he halfway hoped that someone would hit him hard and put him down for good.

Finally Ted's parents and his doctor persuaded him to go to the Veteran's Administration (VA) hospital. There he was diagnosed as having a stress syndrome and urged to get into a veterans' group for counseling. But before Ted could get involved with the counseling group, he got drunk and drove his car onto the VA hospital grounds and ripped up the golf practice green. He was arrested, faced a federal court judge, and was given a suspended sentence, providing he entered the VA alcohol treatment unit.

Ted went through the eight-week treatment course, learned he was an addict, learned he'd have to stay away from alcohol and other drugs for the rest of his life. Ted was twenty-five years old, and the prospect of staying away from alcohol for the rest of his life didn't fill him with enthusiasm. In the real world — the world outside the hospital grounds — his social life was in the taverns. The only friends he had were drinking buddies, and, more importantly to Ted, his only contact with women was in bars. He had never been able to muster up courage to date a woman when he was sober. He had never had sex when he was drug-free.

On his release from the VA, Ted went into a halfway house and was encouraged to seek work. He was broke, had no work skills, and had no stable work history outside of his infantry training for combat. Nevertheless, Ted had definite ideas about work. He didn't know what he wanted to do, but he had very strong feelings about what he *wasn't* going to do. "I'm not gonna take a minimum wage job," Ted said bitterly. "I'm better than that."

Ted had an attitude problem.

Over a period of several months, it became clear that no one was going to pay Ted what he thought he was worth, so he eventually began working at a minimum wage job just to regain a sense of self-sufficiency. He had to swallow his false pride, and he eventually conceded that it was better to have minimum wage than no wage at all.

With the help of a counselor, Ted began to learn how to control his anxiety around women. He learned to talk with them, to joke with them, and he gradually realized that casual conversation did not mean sexual invitation.

In short, Ted learned to relax and be more casual about

himself. He began to get his mind off himself and to see that other people had problems and feelings. He began to develop empathy.

"I still have nightmares occasionally," Ted reflects. "But, then, who doesn't? I met a guy in AA who has bad nightmares about college. He wakes up sweating, about ready to have a heart attack because it's the end of the term and he hasn't studied and he can't find the room where the final exam is being held."

Ted still has some bitter thoughts about Vietnam. But he also knows now how fortunate he was. "I got out without getting wounded. I didn't get hit with Agent Orange. I've got a lot of things to be thankful for. About the best thing I ever did was to stop feeling sorry for myself and get on with my life."

Ted stays sober now. He's been steadily employed as a night watchman for the past five years. He started out at minimum wage and has worked up to a position of seniority with the company. He attends AA, and he has a steady girlfriend.

He occasionally returns to the VA hospital for a "refresher course." It hasn't been easy, but then he's learned the hard way that a lot of important things in life don't come easy.

All excellent things are as difficult as they are rare.

— Spinoza

CHAPTER SEVEN

Using Drugs to Treat Anxiety

Tranquilizers enable people to persist in their ordinary activities while leading lives of howling desperation.
— *Marshall McLuhan*

We must recognize the vital necessity of being clean and sober before we can deal with our other life problems. But we must also recognize that some recovering people may benefit from prescription medication to deal with anxiety — especially disabling anxiety disorders.

This can be confusing for us, especially when we know that many drugs prescribed for anxiety, depression, and other emotional problems are addictive, which means they can be poison for recovering alcoholics, other addicts, and codependents.

Current research shows that major anxiety disorders may be biochemical — that is, physical, rather than mental — in origin. If this is true, we are faced with a difficult question. Should recovering alcoholics, other addicts, and codependents — people who are highly susceptible to chemical abuse — use psychoactive medications to treat anxiety?

This is a very controversial subject. Some recovering folks insist that psychoactive medications should *never* be used under any circumstances. Others believe that the judicious use of medication can be useful to treat anxiety, depression, and other disorders afflicting recovering people.

What Does AA Say?*

Alcoholics Anonymous has taken an official position on the use of psychoactive medications by AA members, which is outlined in the pamphlet, *The A.A. Member — Medications and Other Drugs*. This compassionate point of view can be of great use to us.

Because of the difficulties that many alcoholics have with drugs, some members have taken the position that no one in A.A. should take any medication. While this position has undoubtedly prevented relapses for some, it has meant disaster for others.

A.A. members and many of their physicians have described situations in which depressed patients have been told by A.A.'s [sic] to throw away the pills, only to have depression return with all its difficulties, some-times resulting in suicide. We have heard, too, from schizophrenics, manic depressives, epileptics, and others requiring medication that well-meaning A.A. friends often discourage them from taking prescribed medication. Unfortunately, by following a layman's advice, the sufferers find that their conditions can return with all their previous intensity. On top of that, they feel guilty because they are convinced that "A.A. is against pills."

It becomes clear that just as it is wrong to enable or support any alcoholic to become readdicted to any drug, it's equally wrong to deprive any alcoholic of medication which can alleviate or control other dis-abling physical and/or emotional problems.

*The A.A. Member — Medications and Other Drugs, New York: Alcoholics Anonymous World Services, Inc., 1984, 9. Reprinted with permission of A.A. World Services, Inc.

Anti-Anxiety Drugs

The drugs currently most in use for treating anxiety disorders are:

- The benzodiazepines (minor tranquilizers, such as Valium, Xanax, Librium, Dalmane, Tranxene, Oxazepam, Serax, Dormalin, Restoril, and Halcion — to name just a few of the major brand names).
- Tricyclic antidepressants, such as imipramine (Tofranil), amitriptyline (Elavil), and other brand names.
- Monamine-oxidase (MAO) inhibitors, such as Nardil, Marplan, and Parnate.
- Beta-blockers such as propanolol — chiefly the brand name Inderal — are sometimes prescribed for social phobia or performance anxiety.

We are opposed to the use of benzodiazepines (minor tranquilizers) by recovering people except in emergency situations under the direct supervision of a medical person. Why such a strong stand? Two reasons:

1. These drugs have a high potential for abuse and addiction.

2. Recovering alcoholics and other addicts have a high potential for readdiction to drugs like these. Non-addicted codependents with a family history of chemical dependency also have a high potential for addiction to these drugs.

Far too many recovering people who would never dream of getting drunk or using illegal drugs become physical and emotional wrecks from using legally prescribed tranquilizers. They had no intention of abusing these drugs, yet they still developed serious problems. Remember: No one ever *intends* to get addicted to alcohol or other drugs.

Shut Up and Take Your Valium*

It is refreshing to find physicians who will speak out candidly against the overuse of minor tranquilizers. Drs. Tom Rusk and Randy Read make no bones about the dangers of "anti-complaint drugs" like Valium:

Doctors know that prescribing tranquilizers, sedatives, and even anti-depressants can cause unhappy patients to become pleasantly quiet. To us, the risk of such legal addictions is extreme. Research into chemical warfare agents may be frightening but it's not nearly so scary as the development of anti-complaint drugs that work "too well."

"Valium" is a good example. . . . Next to alcohol, it is probably the most widely abused drug in this country. It makes people feel relaxed, dissolves anxiety, and gives a "high" reminiscent of a stiff shot of booze. For certain psychiatric conditions, where anxiety is truly debilitating, diazepam [Valium] can be a life saver. But that's not how it is used much of the time. Valium eaters, like the lotus eaters of Greek mythology, use the drug to forget, to get by, to cope, to slide through . . . instead of waking up and doing something. It's one of the most popular ways to avoid psychological pain — why change when you can get a little high? And once again, busy physicians often use Valium and drugs like it to get patients to shut up. Patients complain of this or that — and a widespread tendency is to give "medications" until they stop complaining. . . .

Most people will never develop full blown addictions but subtle dependencies may occur. Using tranquilizers even "just to get through a crisis" may cut back our ability to cope on our own. Who knows? Many people who frequently take Valium may be undergoing a gradual shift toward permanent dullness or chronic fearfulness. Their slow decline may not become obvious for another decade. As a nation, we overuse chemicals so habitually that subtle destructive effects can go unnoticed for years.

*I Want to Change, But I Don't Know How! Tom Rusk, M.D. and Randy Read, M.D., Los Angeles: Price/Stern/Sloane,1980.

Pills & Perfection*

And here's what physician Alan Klass has to say about our long and persistent cultural quest for perfection through pills:

The rapid rate of technological progress inevitably leads to the belief that for every situation relief is readily available. For every need there must be fulfilment. To many, this is what is meant by rising standards of living.

But with rising expectations come the tensions and the struggles for fulfilment. We have been led to believe that for every disease there is a remedy. We expect and demand freedom from any form of anxiety or psychological tension. In short, we demand to feel good throughout the wakeful part of the day, to sleep soundly at night, and to awaken refreshed, full of zeal and the eagerness to cope. We demand total freedom from any pain or discomfort, even for the shortest period. The "common cold" is no longer tolerable. We expect the anxieties that come with the tests of life, the examination, the interview, the decision, the marriage, the bereavement, and so on, to be made free from discomfort and dis-ease.

We have been taught and conditioned to believe that these rough situations can be made smooth by the appropriate medications. . . .

We have become conditioned to accept that there is indeed a state of perfect health. Our notion of what is "normal" centers around this concept of blooming, perfect health. . . . In pursuing this ideal we are quick to accept any nostrum, any treatment that promises quickly to remove the occasional discomfort or the periodic transient illness.

There's Gold in Them Thar Pills: An Inquiry into the Medical-Industrial Complex, Alan Klass, New York: Penguin Books, 1975.

In their book, *The Tranquilizing of America*, Richard Hughes and Robert Brewin warn:

> Medical research in the 1970s has turned up alarming evidence that the tranquilizers are not the safe, benign substances that many doctors and many patients believed them to be. Probably the most pernicious effect of this class of drugs is on the mind. Although they do, to use a phrase that many former pillheads used to relish, "take the edge off" anxiety, pain, and stress, they also take the edge off life itself. All these substances act on the one organ that truly differentiates man from animals: the mind. Even the person who uses tranquilizers only in the manner his physician recommends is making a trade-off that should be questioned — these pills not only numb the pain but numb the whole mind.

It is the deepest conviction of the authors that for recovering alcoholics, other addicts, and codependents, the risks of using tranquilizers far outweigh the potential benefits.

Whose Responsibility?

It is the recovering person's responsibility to make this point clear to well-meaning physicians who try to help with a prescription for any of the many different brands of tranquilizers, sleeping pills, and other sedative drugs.

Two guidelines for self-protection:

1. Tell your doctor that you're in recovery.

2. Do not accept a prescription for an anti-anxiety drug or a muscle relaxant or a sleeping pill

without getting from your doctor a complete explanation of the prescribed drug.

We need not be reluctant to question either the doctor or pharmacist. It is their professional obligation to answer our questions. While it is the medical person's responsibility to give us information, it is our responsibility to ask questions if the information isn't freely offered in terms we can understand. We may feel shy about questioning a medical professional, yet we must remember that our recovery is certainly worth the effort it takes to dig out this information.

Recommended Anti-Anxiety Medications

What about the tricyclic antidepressants, the MAO inhibitors, and beta-blockers?

Under certain conditions, these drugs can be a boon to anxious and depressed recovering people. Although these drugs are commonly called antidepressants, research shows they are also excellent anti-anxiety agents.

One reason they seem useful for recovering people is that they pose a lower risk for abuse, mostly because they don't have a euphoric drug effect. In other words, they don't make you high.

You may be a candidate for anti-anxiety medication — *supervised by a physician* — if you can answer "yes" to the following questions.

1. Are you unable to carry out your day-to-day activities because of your anxiety and fears?

2. Do you often suffer from physical symptoms such as agitation, racing heart, feelings of paralysis, choking sensations, or inability to breathe right?

3. Are you willing to follow your doctor's prescription to the letter?

4. Are you willing to report all side effects to your doctor?

5. Are you willing to make other changes in your habits, such as reducing your caffeine consumption, that will increase the probability of the medication working for you?

These guidelines are general — not meant to be comprehensive. If you do seek medical help, keep in mind that these drugs often need several weeks to take effect. The dosage may have to be adjusted several times before optimum benefit is reached. And sometimes, the drugs simply won't work for your particular problem.

Without exception, people being treated with drug therapy must stay in close contact with the prescribing physician. If the medication doesn't seem to work, or if you suffer from side effects, let your doctor know. Otherwise, you won't receive the help you want and need.

And if your personal physician refuses or fails to recognize the peculiar susceptibilities of recovering people to sedatives, tranquilizers, and narcotic drugs, you should seriously consider finding a doctor who does understand chemical dependency.

Take as Directed

Although antidepressant drugs are generally considered safe for recovering people, we must remember our habits of excess. While these drugs do not have a euphoric effect, if taken in a large dose they can be stupefying. Some recovering people have doubled, tripled, and quadrupled their prescribed dosage and turned themselves into slobbering zombies.

Even in normal doses these drugs can have unpleasant side effects such as foamy saliva and rapid heartbeat. They can impair sexual responsiveness. *In large doses, they can be life-threatening.*

Paradoxically, some people find these side effects to be so unpleasant that they quit taking the medication that can help them get their anxiety under control.

Important Questions to Consider

All too often, people rush to the quick fix of a drug when they feel bad, and they ignore other ways of combating distress that may in the long run be more effective.

In *Mood Control*, Gene Bylinsky notes the consequences of rushing to medication:

> Statistics show that an astounding one-quarter of all prescriptions written today are for psychotropic drugs — not to treat psychotic or severely depressed patients but relatively normal or mildly neurotic individuals who show symptoms of anxiety, tension, insomnia, slight depression, and other types of mood disturbances often associated with life in modern society.

Before considering medication as an option in your own program of recovery, ask yourself these very important questions:

- *Have I tried alternative ways to reduce my anxiety?* Have I reduced my consumption of caffeine? Am I eating regular meals (and staying away from junk foods)? Am I getting regular exercise? Do I use any calming exercises or other stress management techniques?

- *Have I had a thorough physical examination to rule out physical disorders that cause anxiety?* Be wary of the physician whose first and fastest response to a complaint of anxiety is a refillable prescription for Xanax or Valium.

Finally, if your physician feels that medication would be useful in bringing your anxiety under control, you must consider this question:

- *Am I capable of taking this medication exactly as directed?*

If there is the slightest doubt in your mind, medication may not be for you.

Part Three

Getting Better

*Anxiety avoided, narcotized, or denied can create
a life semi-crippled by psychological symptoms
and illnesses, whereas anxiety understood and
handled properly can stimulate vigorous
personality growth and lead the way to a
meaningful resolution of human problems.*

— *Daniel A. Sugarman, Ph.D.*

CHAPTER EIGHT

A Framework for Getting Better

When we experience physical or emotional distress, most of us want to know why. What's our problem? Why do we feel this way? These "why" questions are important because it's often difficult to remedy physical or emotional distress unless we have a pretty good idea what's causing it.

If a man has chest pains in the night, does he take an antacid for his stomach or a nitroglycerin pill for his heart? Before the man or his doctors decide on treatment, they have to ask that crucial question: Why?

If they answer the question incorrectly, the results can be disastrous.

The same goes for anxiety problems. Should a woman with panic attacks see a psychoanalyst, or should she stop drinking ten cups of coffee a day? That's a vital question. And it's difficult to answer with 100 percent certainty.

When it comes to emotional distress — anxiety, depression, grief, anger — doctors have no absolutely reliable tests to indicate the best course of treatment.

A doctor can look inside the human body and say, "Aha! Your pain is caused by a heart blockage. We have to do surgery."

But there is no miracle machine that can allow a doctor to say with certainty, "Yes, I see clearly your heart has been broken. That's why you're in pain."

Internal & External Triggers

The question of *why* has another complication: Some of our anxiety is a response to *external* events, and some of our anxiety is a response to *internal* events.

External events are fairly easy for us to understand. Picture yourself outside the hospital emergency room waiting to find out if your child has a fractured skull. Or wondering if the mill where you've worked for seventeen years is going to shut down. Or if the blood test is going to come up positive or negative. Or if your ex-husband is going to send child support this month.

Much of the anxiety we feel in response to external events is due to our lack of control over the situation. We don't know what's going to happen. We don't know if we can change the outcome. We feel helpless, angry, and afraid.

Remember the Serenity Prayer: *"God grant me the serenity to accept the things I cannot change . . ."*

If our anxiety is caused by our inability to change or control external circumstances, our recovery approach has to be one of serenity and acceptance. We have to take on the difficult task of Letting Go and Letting God.

Sometimes it's hard to tell if our distress is caused by internal or external events. Often it is a combination of both. Anxiety that's a response to external events only will disappear in a wave of relief if the situation changes for the better — if, for example, the doctor says, "Your child is all right. Just a bump on the head. Nothing to worry about."

If the anxiety continues even when events around us are working out, or if our anxiety is out of proportion to the situation, we are probably responding to internal cues. What are these cues?

Thoughts   Values
Beliefs   Biochemistry

Negative thinking, making mountains out of molehills, perfectionism, and the idea that we should always look good in the eyes of others — these are just a few of the internal events that can trigger anxiety.

There's also a connection between our internal *physical* processes and anxiety. Much of our anxiety occurs because our biochemistry gets knocked seriously out of whack by disease, alcohol and other drug abuse, severe stress, excessive dieting or other poor eating habits, and for reasons that are simply beyond medical comprehension.

The Serenity Prayer also says: *God grant me "the courage to change the things I can . . ."*

If our anxiety is triggered even in part by internal events, our recovery program has to be one of action and positive efforts to change our thinking and our lifestyles. With practice, self-understanding, and honesty, we can learn to change the destructive thoughts and beliefs that turn us into emotional wrecks. We can also do a lot to balance our messed-up biochemistry through changes in our lifestyle and with professional therapeutic assistance.

Where to Start

Unfortunately, some therapists can become quite dogmatic in their attachment to a particular theory of human emotion. They may insist that all adult distress stems from childhood trauma and that the only solution is through long-term therapy aimed at getting insight into unconscious conflicts.

Other therapists may think that every twisted emotion comes from a twisted molecule, so their only approach is through medication or diet or other biochemical tinkering.

Human beings are complex creatures, and explanations of our behavior don't come in one-size-fits-all packages. No one explanation fits all the ups and downs and loop-de-loops of our emotions.

Those of us who want to reach our highest potential will be wise to paint the road signs on our journey to recovery with a broad brush. We don't have to pick one route only.

Human beings are predictable. We find it hard to resist immediate gratification. Most of us simply don't have the patience to keep plugging away at our personal problems unless we see some benefits coming our way right from the start. That's one reason so many people drop out of long-term therapy. It takes a long time to get results, and progress is often excruciatingly slow.

Any form of therapy can provide some relief, even if

On Oversimplification*

Man is a multiple amphibian who lives in about twenty different worlds at once. If anything is to be done to improve his *enjoyment* of life, to improve the way he can realize his desirable potentialities, to improve his health, to improve the quality of his relations with other people, to improve his *morality*, we have to attack on all fronts at once.

And the greatest, and what may be called the original sin of the human mind is *sloth*, it's over-simplification. We *want* to think that there is only one cause for every given phenomenon, therefore there is only one cure — *there is not!* This is the trouble: no phenomenon on the human level, which is a level of immense complexity, can ever have a single cause — we must always take at least a half a dozen conspiring factors into consideration. . . .

*Aldous Huxley, quoted in 1960, from *Aldous Huxley: A Biography*, Sybille Bedford, New York: Knopf and Harper & Row, 1973.

---

only temporary. Some people who seek help want to be reassured they're not crazy. Others find comfort in being able to talk with a friend or a professional about emotional distress.

Therapy can help many people, but therapy works best when it's a partnership for change.

Therapy Junkies & Insight Addicts

Therapy junkies are people who jump from one therapist to another. They come up with insight after insight into their maladies, but once the insight is gained, nothing changes, and they become disenchanted with that particular brand of therapy. Then they move on to another brand — one that promises new insights, new explanations for the continuing distress.

Even the most plausible or satisfying insight can be wrong. And even if the insight is right, we still have to make changes in our present lives in order to relieve distress.

One of the ways we deceive ourselves is to think that if we find the "real" psychological reasons for our behavior, then our insight will automatically resolve our problems. In the past, this attitude was one of the prime obstacles to recovery from addiction. Professionals once firmly believed that alcoholism and other addictions were symptoms of an underlying disorder — unresolved conflicts. Once the underlying disorder was cleared up, a person would no longer have to use alcohol, and could probably become a social drinker.

Treatment of alcoholism and other addictions was a resounding flop.

Largely due to the influence of AA, alcoholism became recognized as a disorder that needed to be addressed directly. It was necessary to devise a program to help the alcoholic quit drinking, instead of trying to discover the underlying reasons for drinking.

Just as there are many reasons why people become dependent on alcohol and other drugs, there are many reasons to be fearful and anxious. And we often feel if we find the reason, then our anxiety will diminish or go away entirely. Our search for reasons may be a kind of interminable quest, sometimes involving perpetual therapy. We may become therapy junkies, always seeking a new and more satisfying explanation for our distress, but seldom taking the steps beyond insight necessary to relieve distress.

So it isn't always helpful to search for the reasons. The reasons we find may seem persuasive and convincing, but they may not have any real connection with our anxiety. More important, knowing the reason doesn't make the anxiety go away. Especially if we believe that anxiety comes only from past, or only from unresolved psychological conflict. Many things can cause anxiety, as can be seen in the box on misdiagnosis on the opposite page.

Important note: *Sometimes self-help is not enough.* Start any therapy program by getting a physical examination from a physician.

Start with the Body

The recovery approach we recommend takes into account our bodies, our ability to think and use our minds, and the reality of painful, unconscious, emotional conflicts.

We think the *body* is the best place to start a personal recovery plan, especially for people who have alcohol and other drug problems.

Why? Chiefly because anxiety is often a *physical* reaction to all the chemical, emotional, dietary, and spiritual abuses we heap upon ourselves. The symptoms of anxiety —

Misdiagnosis of Anxiety*

Dr. Mark Gold warns about jumping to conclusions about the causes of anxiety. He gives three examples of misdiagnosis:

Trip was a cheerful, cooperative five-year-old boy. Then shortly before he started kindergarten, he grew restless and timid. On the first day of class he was terrified and screamed hysterically until his mother took him home. After two weeks of this unusual behavior, his parents took him to a child psychiatrist who diagnosed Trip as having school phobia. There was no improvement after six weeks of therapy. A routine physical examination later showed that Trip was suffering from Wilson's disease — a rare metabolic disorder that can cause anxiety and school phobia. Therapy failed because Trip needed treatment for a physical disease.

Linda moved from a small town to a large city. About six months later, she was struck by intense feelings of fear and dread while attending a play. Her heart pounded furiously, she couldn't get her breath, and she felt like she was going to die. After ten minutes, the attack passed. Linda had four more attacks in the next three weeks. Afraid she was losing her mind, Linda consulted a psychiatrist. He told her she was having panic attacks and prescribed antidepressant medication. But her panic attacks continued. It turned out that Linda was suffering from an endocrine disorder, pheochromocytoma. Symptoms of this disease mimic the symptoms of a panic attack. Linda's disease would be helped by surgery, not by medication for panic.

Andy's fear of strangers started in an elevator, but soon he began to feel anxiety on buses and in restaurants. He began to avoid places where he might encounter strangers. He found it hard to go to work. His psychiatrist diagnosed Andy's problem as xenophobia — an abnormal fear of strangers — and prescribed psychotherapy. Andy's fears worsened. What went wrong? Andy worked in a plant that manufactured mercury-vapor lamps. His symptoms of heightened anxiety and xenophobia weren't "psychological" at all. He was suffering from work-related mercury poisoning.

Dr. Gold sums up problems of misdiagnosis: "There are no symptoms associated with *only* mental disorders. Even some of the most bizarre patterns of behavior and thinking can be traced to biological sources."

* Adapted from *The Good News About Panic, Anxiety & Phobias*, Mark Gold, New York: Villard Books, 1989.

pounding heart, sweating, breathing difficulties, and so on — can be the physical and emotional manifestations of a body chemistry thrown seriously out of whack by a self-destructive lifestyle. Changes in behavior can often rebalance our body chemistry and produce a rapid reduction of anxiety symptoms. And that's important to anyone who is suffering.

There's also another reason. If you are serious about recovery, you've already taken the first step in balancing your biochemistry — you have detoxed from alcohol and other intoxicating drugs. That's an important step, but it's only the beginning. Many of us may be experiencing anxiety created by our use of other perfectly legal and acceptable drugs. One of the best kept secrets of human psychology is that many mental problems are caused by the consumption of ordinary substances. We may find that some of us who are alcohol- and drug-free still have some detoxing to do.

Drug-Induced Anxiety

In *Handbook of Anxiety Disorders*, Alan Lipschitz states: "By far the most frequent causes of anxiety are drug intoxication and withdrawal from alcohol or other drugs."

What's the most common drug source of drug-induced anxiety? *Caffeine.* That's right, good old java — coffee — the drug most Americans use to get going in the morning and to fend off the mid-afternoon doldrums.

Caffeine is well known as the main psychoactive chemical in coffee. Caffeine is perhaps the most widely used stimulant in the United States, and daily overdoses of caffeine by law-abiding adults may be one of the most widespread and least-acknowledged forms of drug abuse. Long-term heavy use creates tolerance, and coffee addicts regularly report withdrawal effects when deprived of their favorite drug.

Most people don't realize the widespread prevalence of caffeine in foods, beverages, and medications. Coffee is not the only source of caffeine. Tea, cola drinks (and other non-cola soft drinks), chocolate bars, and cocoa — all contain caffeine. Caffeine is included in many over-the-counter medications, including headache remedies (Anacin), stimulants (No Doz), cold and allergy preparations (Dristan), appetite suppressants, and other drugs.

Caffeinism

Psychologist John B. Murray describes what occurs when people consume excessive amounts of caffeine-containing substances: "Caffeinism may develop when daily ingestion reaches more than 500 to 600 mgs of caffeine, an amount equivalent to 4 to 7 or more cups of coffee or 7 to 9 cups of tea in a day." Symptoms of caffeinism sound almost exactly like anxiety symptoms: Nervous irritability, tremulousness, muscle twitches, insomnia, heart palpitations, flushing (turning red in the face), irregular heartbeat, and gastrointestinal disturbances.

Alan Lipschitz points out that people suffering from anxiety "commonly are unaware of the large doses of caffeine they habitually ingest in sodas, coffee, and headache remedies; this use can produce a state of chronic recurrent caffeine intoxication. When the caffeine addict deliberately or unwittingly stops ingesting the drug, anxiety may be experienced as one symptom of the caffeine withdrawal syndrome, which typically also includes headache and lethargy."

In a 1974 paper, "Anxiety or Caffeinism: A Diagnostic Dilemma," psychiatrist J. F. Greden identified caffeinism as a common clinical syndrome: "Caffeinism probably can be found among a fairly large percentage of patients with psychiatric symptoms, especially those with mixed anxiety/depression profiles."

Caffeine can not only cause anxiety, it can also intensify the symptoms already present in people who have panic attacks or other forms of anxiety.

Psychiatrist Mark Gold warns: "While caffeine has been shown to induce panic attacks in panic disorder patients, it can also produce panic in individuals with no history of panic attacks. Approximately ten cups of coffee will produce a panic attack in normal subjects."

Heavy coffee drinkers often smoke — which places a double burden on the nervous system because the nicotine in tobacco is also a stimulant that can cause or intensify anxiety.

So the two most common drugs in our culture — caffeine and nicotine — turn out to be drugs that make us anxious. If we want to reduce our feelings of nervousness and prevent intense anxiety, we can start at the obvious places: Reducing coffee consumption and quit smoking.

The Drug Withdrawal Effect

The *Handbook of Anxiety Disorders* indicates that withdrawal from alcohol is the single most common physical cause of anxiety. Narcotic withdrawal (heroin or methadone) also triggers anxiety. Withdrawal from alcohol or narcotics can cause anxiety within hours of discontinuing the drug, but symptoms may also occur days later.

Those are the most widely known forms of withdrawal-induced anxiety, but withdrawal from any addicting drug can produce anxiety. It's been known for many years that "rebound anxiety" occurs after ceasing almost any minor tranquilizer. This, again, is one of the ironies of drug use. We use minor tranquilizers like Valium, Librium, or Xanax to help us manage our anxiety, only to discover that our anxiety increases if we stop using the drug. This is a model for chemical dependency.

And it doesn't happen only in withdrawal from minor tranquilizers. Cigarette smokers say that smoking calms their nerves, but it does so by feeding the addiction and by briefly satisfying the craving for nicotine during withdrawal.

Drug use and drug withdrawal — these two common sources of anxiety must be considered whenever we are stricken with panic or suffer episodes of anxiety that seem to happen "for no reason at all."

CHAPTER NINE

Stress-Busters for Mood & Morale

If a person suffers a heart attack or gets an ulcer or even if he or she comes down with a bad case of the flu, one of the first questions we ask is, "Was he under a lot of stress?" That question shows that almost all of us realize the relationship between stress and health. Too much of the wrong kind of stress can cause the body to start self-destructing.

But what does the word *stress* really mean?

Most of us use it to describe intense, negative emotional experiences, such as family problems, job problems, illness, or financial difficulties. But stress is not some external event that happens to us. Stress is internal. It involves our bodies and minds.

What Is Stress?

The body tends to maintain a steady internal balance despite changes in the environment. If the internal balance is disrupted, the body immediately reacts, attempting to restore balance and stability. The body's balancing act is called *homeostasis*. In other words, homeostasis is the body's tendency to maintain a steady state despite changes in the external environment. *Any failure in homeostasis results in physical or emotional illness.*

Stress, then, can be seen as any disruption of the homeostasis of the body. Chronic stress can lead to serious physical and emotional illness.

Stress always involves the physiological reactions of the body. It always means there's a disturbance in the body's balancing act.

And since the body bone's connected to the head bone, stress involves our emotions and thoughts.

Whatever causes the stress is called the *stressor*. For example, an ugly disagreement with your boss is a stressor. Your internal physical and emotional reaction to the disagreement is the stress. If your homeostatic mechanisms jump around like water on a hot griddle, you're under a lot of stress. If you really don't care, if your internal reaction is minimal, then your stress level is also minimal.

The Stressors in Your Life

Most of the serious stressors modern people face are non-physical. That is, we don't spend much time outrunning bears or trying to eke out an existence scratching roots from drought-parched soil. Instead, we're stressed by threats to our social survival and well-being. What is social stress? It's whatever a person perceives it to be.

This is an old idea, ancient wisdom even at the time when a Roman philosopher wrote: "We fear not so much the things themselves, but rather our idea of things." In other words, our reaction to a nonphysical stressor depends more on our perception of the situation, rather than on the reality of the situation.

We often feel stressed out if events don't live up to our preconceived ideas of how they should be. Danny and Myrna are a good example of how expectations can lead to stress.

Danny's chemical dependency practically ruined his marriage. Finally, he entered treatment and got sober and straight. He felt really good about himself, proud of his accomplishments, and he expected his wife, Myrna, to feel the same way. He thought she would praise him to her relatives and friends. He also expected her to automatically want him to become the "man of the house" once again. And as the reinstated head of the household, Danny thought he should make all the major decisions.

Myrna had other ideas. She told Danny she wasn't terribly impressed by his mere two months of sobriety after ten years of drinking. She held tight to the family finances and told Danny he would have to "prove himself" awhile longer before she would be ready to trust him.

Danny was outraged. How could Myrna be such a selfish, castrating witch? As they argued, his face turned red, his hands shook, his heart beat like mad, and his stomach was a tight knot. He also craved a drink. Later, as Danny stewed about how unfairly he was being treated, he felt nervous and crawly all over. His mouth was dry and his skin hurt. He was surprised. He thought that getting sober would put an end to all these problems.

Obviously there was a big conflict between Danny's expectations and reality. His emotional reaction took the form of a severe stress response. The stressors were twofold:

1. The arguments with his wife, *and*
2. His unrealistic expectations.

These two stressors created Danny's emotional reaction. And the emotions, in turn, generated distressing physical reactions. Anytime we experience intense emotions such as anger, frustration, or fear, a number of specific, predictable physiological changes take place in the body.

This is important for us to understand because recovery increases our capacity to experience the full range of normal emotions. That's why in recovery we may actually feel more stressed out than in the days when we wandered around numb. Part of our recovery effort has to include learning how to cope with the stress that comes with being a fully alert and alive being.

Fight or Fearful Flight

When we are angry or frightened, our autonomic nervous system becomes excited and stimulates the release of hormones in the body. One of these hormones is adrenalin, which begins to mobilize the body for strenuous physical activity. The outpouring of adrenalin causes a rapid rise in the blood sugar level so that the muscles will have a good supply of energy. This entire process is called the *fight-or-flight response*. It's been with us for millions of years and can both help and harm us.

THE FIGHT-OR-FLIGHT RESPONSE

**The automatic reaction of the body during
anger or fear. The response causes an
outpouring of hormones that increases
heart rate, respiration, blood pressure, and
metabolism. It also causes a rapid increase
in the blood sugar level.**

This response can be lifesaving if we are fighting off or running from an attacker. It also explains how a mother can lift a five hundred-pound weight off her child in an emergency without blinking an eye.

Unfortunately, we may trigger this stressful response when we hit every red light on the way to work.

This repeated stress can disrupt the body's chemical balance, throw our system out of kilter, and thus result in physical illness, depression, irritability, and anxiety. *These bad feelings can lead a recovering person directly to relapse.*

If the body chronically responds to insignificant situations with the fight-or-flight response, we can really start feeling awful. Stress can cause symptoms of distress or intensify them. Here's just a partial list of stress-related problems:

Insomnia   Asthma
Anxiety   Heart disease
Headaches   High blood pressure
Ulcers   Hypoglycemia
Colitis   Diabetes
Depression   Immune system disorders
Alcoholism   Drug addiction
            Codependent behaviors

The Red Alert Nervous System

There's considerable scientific evidence that addiction — especially alcoholism — runs in families. There is an increasing body of evidence that a *susceptibility* to addiction may be an inherited trait. Research has shown that the children of alcoholics are more likely to have alcohol problems than the children from non-alcoholic families, even when the children are separated from their alcoholic parents at birth and raised in families with no drinking problems.

Now consider this: Some people may possess nervous systems that for unknown physical reasons stay on *RED ALERT!* when they should be at ease. Some of us may be born more tightly strung than the average person, reacting more intensely to sensations — light and sound and touch. Stimulation barely noticed by the average person may be highly irritating to someone with a red alert nervous system.

Scientists are investigating the possibility that this type of tension and nervousness may stem from a genetic trait passed on from generation to generation. At this point, there isn't enough scientific evidence to clearly state that addictions and a super-sensitive nervous system are biochemically related, but many recovering people report they were always a little more sensitive, a little more nervous, a little more touchy than the average person. This was true before they became chemically dependent and after they got sober and straight.

So it's possible that many recovering people may have to struggle with over-sensitive nerves because they were born with a red alert nervous system.

And the children of alcoholics (even those who do not develop addiction problems of their own) may be hit with a double whammy — the destructive effects of growing up in a troubled family *and* the risk of having inherited a nervous system predisposed to anxiety.

Taking Time for Stress-Busters

Simple techniques of meditation or prayer can actually help us gain control over the fight-or-flight response. But it takes practice.

For best results, you need to set aside two twenty-minute sessions a day. Before you reach in despair for a crumpet, crying, "I don't have that much time!" — take a moment to consider just how much time you do have.

- How much time did you used to spend drinking, doing other drugs, or trying to change things you couldn't change?
- What are you doing with the time now?
- Is your recovery worth forty minutes a day? . . . Even twenty minutes a day?

The Moment of Truth: HAVING TIME IS TAKING TIME.

Getting in the Mood

You can learn to control your reaction to stress by using a simple, but effective, technique of meditation. If you don't like the word *meditation*, you can call it a relaxation exercise. You need four conditions to promote success.

1. *A Quiet Place*: Is there a place you can go, away from the kids, the TV, and the phone? You won't be able to relax much if you have interruptions, so maybe you will have to ask for the cooperation of your family for a few minutes each day.

2. *Something to Focus Your Mind On*: A key word, a sound, a mental picture. By focusing your mind

on one particular thing, you will be able to prevent your mind from wandering toward distressing thoughts. If your mind begins to wander, gently pull it back by concentrating on your word or image.

3. *A Passive Attitude*: Forget about how well you are performing. If you try too hard at relaxing, you will just become more tense. Let your body relax. If your mind wanders away from your key word or image, don't become upset. Just let the relaxation happen.

4. *A Comfortable Position*: Find a position that allows you to relax all of your muscles, but don't get so comfortable that you fall asleep.

There are many effective relaxation and meditation techniques. If you already use a method that works for you, stick with it. Transcendental meditation, yoga, and prayer are all good ways of relaxing the body and setting the mind at ease. Dr. Herbert Benson developed a simple technique called *The Relaxation Response* that is both effective and easy to learn. The technique we suggest is adapted from Dr. Benson's book *Beyond the Relaxation Response*.

Read through the following exercise, sit back, relax your body, and give it a try. Remember: Any new skill takes practice. You may not become totally relaxed on your first or second try, but if you keep at it, you will find that relaxation becomes easier each time.

A Relaxation Exercise

1. Find a quiet place and get into a comfortable position.

2. Close your eyes.

3. Relax all the muscles of your body, from your feet on up to your head. Let your whole body feel relaxed, heavy, and comfortable.

4. When your whole body feels relaxed, focus all your attention on your breathing. Feel each breath as it goes in . . . and . . . out.

5. Now, as you inhale each breath, silently repeat the word *calm* to yourself. With each breath, silently repeat the word *calm*. Breathe at your natural, normal pace.

6. Continue relaxing, repeating the word *calm* with each breath for the next ten to twenty minutes.

7. After ten or twenty minutes, again focus all your attention on your breathing. Then repeat the following sentence: "Each time I feel tense, nervous, or uptight, I will think of the word *calm* and I *will* be calm."

8. Repeat the above sentence silently to yourself several times.

9. When you are finished, sit quietly for a few minutes.

Don't worry about whether you were able to achieve a really deep level of relaxation. If you try too hard, you will get more tense. Obviously, we don't want you to try so hard that you end up becoming *more* tense and anxious.

And if your mind wanders away from the word *calm*, don't be too concerned. It's perfectly normal at first. *You will get better with practice.* When you notice other thoughts creeping into your head, just turn them aside and again focus on your breathing, and repeat the word *calm*.

What Good Will Meditation Do Me?

An immediate reaction to meditation is decreased fight-or-flight activity in the autonomic nervous system — which means that your heart rate goes down, your blood pressure goes down, and your muscles relax. An especially important effect is a decrease in a substance called *blood lactate*, a chemical produced by the metabolism of the skeletal muscles.

High blood lactate levels cause a feeling of anxiety. And during the first ten minutes of meditation, the lactate levels fall dramatically. *This means that meditation can physically reduce feelings of anxiety.*

Regular practice of meditation can also reduce high blood pressure, help relieve tension and headaches, stabilize blood sugar levels, and prevent or cure insomnia.

These benefits call for a word of warning. Regular meditation may decrease the amount of medication you need to control any of the above conditions.

If you are under a physician's care, let your physician know what you are doing, so she can make any appropriate adjustments in your medication. This is particularly important if you are under treatment for hypertension.

The One-Minute Stress-Buster

If we regularly practice relaxation exercises and use the word *calm*, we can develop a powerful tool to use in stressful situations. By silently repeating the word *calm* when we feel ourselves starting to lose our cool, we can evoke what is called a conditioned emotional response. *Calm* becomes a cue for the nervous system to relax.

Try this: When you find yourself in a tense situation, take a sixty-second break. Breathe deeply and silently repeat the word *calm*. If you have been regularly practicing the ten-to twenty-minute relaxation exercise, this one-minute stress-buster can really work wonders.

To be effective, the relaxation exercise must be practiced each day. The calming effect of the relaxation exercise will wear off in a very short time if not used regularly.

On Meditation, Relaxation & Miracles

Meditation and other stress management techniques can be useful for relieving tension and anxiety — no question about it. Even the slogans used by many AA members can be cues for relaxation — reminders to Take It Easy, Keep It Simple, One Day at a Time, Easy Does It, and so on. Some folks find that affirmations help during stressful times.

But there may come a time when you might have to consider changing parts of your life that bring chronic tensions and anxiety. There are real stressors in our lives that simply won't go away, no matter how much we meditate, no matter how many books of affirmations we memorize.

Don Ardell, author of *High Level Wellness*, warns:

> There are objective conditions in some of our lives that deserve evaluation and possible reconstruction. You may become the most skilled meditator in the looney bin if you do nothing over the years about a tension-producing job or a profession you abhor, a husband/wife/mate who will always drive

you up a proverbial wall (and vice versa, which is just as distress-provoking), or some other disabling stress producer.

The point is this: Meditation is a valuable tool for helping us cope with the unavoidable stress of everyday life. But it's not magic. Sometimes we have to do the difficult job of *changing the things we can.*

Fitness & Recovery

Some form of exercise or physical fitness training should be a key element in any recovery program. Physical activity is an excellent way to loosen up, to relieve stress, to relax.

More: Research shows that *fitness* relieves symptoms of depression, improves self-image, develops social skills and cognitive functioning, and reduces anxiety and physiological responses to stressors.

Many treatment programs now recommend physical exercise as a way to improve mood (lower anxiety and depression) and as part of relapse prevention training. If you are interested in getting your body and head into shape, consider getting at least fifteen to twenty minutes of moderate physical activity every day.

The I-Hate-to-Jog Guide to Fitness

Do I have to jog?
Jogging and running are popular but highly overrated paths to physical fitness. While there's no question that running can improve fitness, running can also cause leg, knee, and ankle injuries. There are even cases of running addiction where commitment to running interfered with work, family, social relationships, and health.

So you don't have to start off by jogging or running. You don't have to qualify for a triathlon. You don't have to undergo a torturous schedule of Iron Man or aerobic workouts.

Walking is one of the best (and most underrated) ways to get started on the road to fitness. Start with a leisurely stroll. Work up to a brisk twenty-minute walk three or four times a week. Or, if nothing else, take the stairs instead of the elevator.

Light aerobics workouts can be beneficial — and they have the added benefit of a group environment. Many people don't engage in fitness training simply because running and walking are often solitary activities. Other fitness suggestions: Swimming or riding a bicycle.

Take it easy, but get moving. One of the biggest hazards of recovery is complacency — not following through with the important activities necessary for good health.

*Fitness & Recovery**

A Canadian study tested forty-six men and twelve women who participated in a fitness component of an alcohol treatment program. The fitness training consisted of one-hour sessions of progressively more vigorous activity every morning. Stretching and warm-up exercises were followed by light calisthenics and a twelve-minute walk or run. Sessions ended with cool-down, muscle-toning exercises.

Three months after the patients completed the fitness program, researchers compared their abstinence rates with similar patients who completed treatment but did not participate in the fitness training exercises.

Results showed that recovering individuals who participated in the fitness training program had a greater likelihood of remaining abstinent than those who completed treatment without fitness training.

Other studies report similar results. Those who engage in fitness training show fitness gains similar to non-alcoholics, and they have higher rates of abstinence than those who do not engage in fitness training.

Fitness training may obviously be of significant value in helping to prevent relapse and enhancing recovery.

* "Fitness and Recovery," Patricia A. Murray, *Alcohol Health and Research World,* Fall, 1986.

CHAPTER TEN

Eat Right to Stay Serene

I have discovered in my own life that a commitment to my own spiritual growth and emotional well-being is supported by a commitment to my body. If we don't nurture our body, our evolution as a person is hampered.

— *Stewart Emery*

Basic Body Work: Care & Feeding the Jalopy

Psychologist Stewart Emery reminds us that our body enables us to carry out our dreams. He calls the body "the vehicle of our essence." Unfortunately, the vehicle of our essence too often turns out to be a rattletrap, a hacking, wheezing, back-firing jalopy that can just barely get us out of bed in the morning, much less transport us to Xanadu. Says Emery, "We take much better care of our automobile, which we can trade in, than we do of our body, which we cannot."

Emery continues: "Most of us have a relationship with our body in which we experience being separate from it, and we do everything we can to maintain the separation. We keep it drugged, anesthetized, antihistaminized, alcoholized, and whatever else we can stuff into it to keep it from making its presence felt."

His advice: *Shake hands with your body.*

So how's your body? Jalopy or Ferrari? What kind of fuel do you put in the vehicle of your essence? High-test? Or low-grade, junkyard fuel that makes your vehicle sputter, shake, shudder, and backfire? Is it a smoking heap, long overdue for an overhaul? Would a tune-up help?

The Two-Step Tune-Up

If we're suffering from the emotional and physical distress of anxiety . . .

— *And* if we've treated ourselves pretty roughly over the years,
— *Or* if we think we may have inherited a red alert nervous system . . .

. . . There are two basic nutritional rules to follow if we want to tune up our systems.

Two Cardinal Rules

1. DON'T skip meals, ever.

2. DON'T consume junk, especially sugar and alcohol.

There are specific reasons for these two rules. Skipping meals puts a strain on our already over-abused glucose homeostasis mechanism. It's like trying to run a high performance automobile on gas fumes from an empty tank. If we skip meals, our blood sugar level can drop so low that we start craving a drink or other drugs to make us feel normal again. And that's a major problem in itself.

Junk food, sugar, and alcohol can give us a rapid blood sugar boost, but in a dangerous and unhealthy way. This can be kind of confusing to understand. It seems logical to say, "Well, hey, my blood sugar level is low so I better eat some sugar to bring it back up again." Doctors even tell diabetics (people whose bodies fail to produce enough of the hormone insulin to allow for normal sugar absorption) to carry sugar cubes with them at all times in case of an emergency. Sometimes a diabetic who takes insulin can suffer a blood sugar drop and become dangerously ill. The sugar cubes can reverse this medical emergency.

Listen: Unless your doctor tells you otherwise, the kind of blood sugar instability recovering people experience is a lifestyle problem, not a medical emergency. If you feel shaky from lack of food, eat something wholesome — a piece of fruit, a whole wheat roll, drink a glass of orange juice. Sugar, alcohol, or other drugs will only make you feel worse.

We have several more specific *suggestions* for a nutritional tune-up, but those first two rules are critical.

Tuning Up for the Long Haul

1. Eat at least three evenly spaced, well-balanced meals a day.

2. Consume adequate protein daily. (Rule of thumb to determine adequate protein: Desired body weight divided by two = grams of protein daily.) Protein may be of animal or vegetable origin.

3. Consume fresh fruits and vegetables daily.

4. Use only whole grains. Include legumes (such as peas and beans) and nuts.

5. Totally eliminate: Tobacco and alcohol.

6. Use sparingly: Sugar (white, brown, syrup, honey, molasses, dried fruit), salt, coffee, tea.

7. Suggested: A fruit, vegetable or protein snack between meals and before bedtime.

8. Take a good multiple vitamin-mineral supplement every day.

9. Remember: Chocolate is not a vitamin.

What's a Gram of Protein?

- One egg equals 6 grams of protein.
- One ounce of milk equals one gram of protein (thus, three 8-ounce glasses of milk a day = 24 grams of protein).
- One ounce of meat equals approximately 6 grams of protein.
- A 1-inch cube of cheese equals 4 grams of protein.

Commonsense Suggestions

1. Overweight? Follow the basic rules as outlined above, but limit fat intake.

2. Balance meals with protein foods, fruits, vegetables, and unrefined starches (such as whole wheat bread, rice, beans).

3. Observe how you feel. Don't continue to eat anything that makes you feel bad.

Caution: When you change from a junk food diet to more nutritious and balanced eating patterns, with less sugar, less coffee, and less junk, you may experience withdrawal symptoms for a few days. You may have unusually strong cravings, you may feel very tired and run-down, and you may get headaches.

These feelings usually go away in a few days, so stick with it, and don't medicate yourself with chocolate ice cream.

The following food lists can help you decide which foods to include when you are planning your meals. When in doubt, read the labels to identify the ingredients.

Foods To Favor	Foods To Avoid
Lean meat	Alcohol
Fish	White flour
Poultry	Pastries, candy, pie
Eggs (sparingly)	Cakes, cookies, donuts
Milk	White bread
Cheese (white)	All soft drinks
Plain yogurt	Most breakfast cereals
Whole grains	Ice cream
Fresh fruit	Canned fruit
Fresh vegetables	Processed food
Nuts, seeds, beans	Coffee, tea (caffeine)
Herbal teas	Flavored yogurt
Unsweetened fruit juice	Fruit-flavored drinks
Cottage cheese	Canned vegetables

SugarSugarSugarSugar

In one form or another, sugar is an ingredient in much of the packaged and prepared food we find in the supermarket and in fast-food restaurants. For example, frozen potatoes and hamburger buns often have a dollop of sugar added. Why? Because sugar browns nicely when it's heated, and who would want to eat a limp, ghostly pale French fry or pasty-looking bun? So the sugar is added to make the cooked food more attractive to the consumer.

There's nothing wrong with wanting food to look appetizing. But we run into problems when most of the food we choose to eat is tinkered with in manufacture. Let's face it — one sugar-enhanced potato isn't going to do much harm. It's those potatoes and buns and cups of canned fruit and packaged cereals, stews, and sauces all lumped together and eaten over the course of a day or week or lifetime that does us in. The sugar is often so well-disguised that we don't know it's there.

The average American consumes over 120 pounds of sugar a year. That figure — 120 pounds — represents an average. In reality, not everyone takes in that amount. Some people consume a whole lot less, others a lot more.

Unbelievable as it may sound, it is not uncommon for a recovering person to consume upwards of five hundred pounds of sugar a year.

Sugar Junkies

One recovering woman who worked in a drug treatment center brought a *ten-pound* bag of sugar to the office every Monday to use in her coffee that workweek. And she didn't share it with her co-workers. It was her private stash.

She said, "If I didn't have my sugar, I felt irritable and crawly all over. In my drinking days, I never ate sweets. But when I got sober, I had to have sugar. I went from being an alcohol addict to being a sugar junkie."

Another young woman recovering from addiction drank sixteen bottles of Dr. Pepper a day. This was a dramatic improvement because she no longer smoked dope and stayed drunk for days at a time. But she couldn't understand why she wasn't smoothing out emotionally. She didn't see the connection between her craving for sugar and her continuing distress. This excessive craving for sugar indicates that the body is desperately trying to maintain homeostasis — usually without success.

---

*Sugar & Booze**

All sweetened carbohydrate beverages, such as the cola drinks, and also sugar cane and sugar candy, can be just as serious nutritional offenders as alcohol if they are used in equal excess. Refined sugar is a pure carbohydrate. It contains no vitamins, minerals, or proteins, nothing except calories. It requires thiamin, niacin, and riboflavin to oxidize it. Anyone who drinks, say, 20 coca-colas a day, is nutritionally in about the same situation as one who drinks a pint of whiskey. Of course, the sugar does not cause gastric disturbances, or impaired absorption and utilization of vitamins, but it does increase the requirement for vitamins because of its vitamin-free calories. The sugar loaded dietary supplements are, in this respect, as bad as alcohol.

*"Alcohol and Nutrition: The Diseases of Chronic Alcoholism," Norman Jolliffe, *Alcohol, Science, and Society,* New Haven, Conn.: Quarterly Journal of Studies on Alcohol, 1945.

Special Note for Newly Recovering People

Many of us have the almost uncontrollable urge to "do everything" once we decide on improving ourselves. If we embark on a healthy eating program, we decide we might as well make it a weight-loss program too. "And smoking — hey, I'd better get off the old cancer sticks. And I'm really out of shape, so I'll start training for the Iron Man competition next month. Why not? I feel great, and I've got all this time now that I've been sober for — what? — six weeks."

This is not a good idea for newly recovering people. Why

not? Detoxing from alcohol and other drugs can be stressful and uncomfortable. Learning the ins and outs of recovery is stressful too. Calorie reduction and chemical abstinence all at once create huge feelings of deprivation that can lead directly to a binge.

Try this plan instead: For the first sixty days of your recovery program, do not restrict the *amount* of food you eat. Instead, restrict the *kind* you eat.

If you're hungry, eat. It might even be a good idea to make planned between-meal snacks of fruit and whole-grain bread a regular part of your regimen. This will help restabilize your messed-up blood sugar mechanism.

And if you're thirsty, drink. Recommended beverages: Unsweetened fruit juice, decaffeinated coffee and tea, or sparkling water.

If the sugar (or alcohol and other drug) craving comes on you strong, eat three oranges or three slices of bread and peanut butter or half a chicken or a beef steak and baked potato. Don't worry about calories. You may gain a few pounds during this time, but you can worry about them later. Once you feel strong in your recovery, once your body is healthy again, then you can start worrying about slimming down.

Panic Attacks? — First Things First

Medical research indicates that as little as one spoonful of sugar or one cup of coffee can trigger a panic attack in a susceptible person. Doctors aren't sure why, but they suspect that some people just have a hypersensitivity to these substances. Even a small, seemingly harmless dose can set off all the internal alarms.

So even though most recovering people can drink one or two cups of coffee a day without harm, it would be a good idea for people who experience panic attacks to give up caffeine and sugar completely. This may be the biggest step you can take to help get your panic attacks under control.

One woman who suffered panic attacks from the time she was nineteen until age thirty-eight agrees wholeheartedly: "I went to my doctor and asked for tranquilizers and instead he ordered me to quit drinking coffee. He said he wouldn't even consider medication until I hadn't had any form of caffeine for two weeks. I thought he was nuts. But guess what? No coffee, no panic attacks. Amazing! I didn't need pills after all."

PMS & Caffeine*

Premenstrual Syndrome (PMS) is characterized by nerves, irritability, depression, and other distressing emotional and physical symptoms. There's a growing body of research indicating that PMS and caffeine consumption — including coffee, tea, and cola beverages — are closely linked.

In a study of Chinese nursing students and factory workers, a team of researchers found that women who drank more than 4.5 cups of tea daily were almost ten times more likely to report symptoms of PMS than women who drank no tea or other beverage containing caffeine.

Researchers suggest that women who suffer from PMS may find relief by eliminating caffeine from their diet.

* "Caffeine-containing Beverages and Premenstrual Syndrome in Young Women," Annette McKay Rossignol, *American Journal of Public Health*,1985.

"Nuts Among the Berries"

Whenever we start talking about the dangers of sugar, caffeine, and junk food in the recovering person's diet, someone usually starts making cracks about the "nuts among the berries." The implication is that we must be some sort of left-field, health-nut cases, desperately clinging to a carton of nonfat yogurt while we're picking little green bean sprouts out of our teeth. Otherwise we'd recognize that recovering people just need to eat a "normal" diet and they'll have good health.

What the wisecrackers don't realize is that what's normal to a person who has been affected by chemical dependency is far, far different from what other people might consider normal.

Understand this: *The hallmark of both addiction and codependency is excess.* Excessive eating, excessive dieting. Excessive smoking, drinking, other drugs. Excessive emotion, excessive denial. Excessive anger, excessive fear, excessive repression. Excessive attempts at control and excessive loss of control.

Even after recovery begins, the patterns of excess continue. One recovering woman put it this way: "Before I went into treatment I drank from morning till night and took prescription drugs by the handfuls. I came out of the treatment center clean and sober from drugs, but I smoke three packs of cigarettes a day, drink coffee by the quart, and I shovel in the candy the same way I used to do with pills. I'm just an excessive person. Always have been."

Recovery does not automatically free us of our excessive habits. Unless we make a specific and concerted effort to change our unhealthy lifestyle, we will continually fall back into dangerous habits that make us feel rotten.

The hallmark of a healthy lifestyle is moderation. For us, moderation is a new concept. To achieve it will take planning, practice, and the realization that we must make a conscious effort to choose moderation in our eating habits, our coffee intake, our dieting efforts, and our entire stance toward our health.

We have learned the hard way that moderation does not come easy. After all, most of us have tried to moderate our alcohol and other drug use without success. Wisely, we have made the choice to abstain from intoxicants. But as Overeaters Anonymous points out, people can abstain from drugs, but they can't abstain from food. We must eat to live.

But we can make choices. Every day we can make the effort to live in a healthy style instead of stumbling along on automatic pilot, letting our old, bad habits of excess make the decisions for us.

The hallmark of recovery is making conscious, healthy choices on a consistent, daily basis.

CHAPTER ELEVEN

Finding Freedom from the Past

Calamity John & Jane

A lot of our anxiety is rooted in the past — things that happened to us last year, ten years ago, thirty years ago. All the past injustices, offenses, and wrongs committed against us set up an expectation of calamity. We're afraid to relax, afraid to risk happiness because past experience warns us that disaster is right around the corner.

Sometimes an impeccable lifestyle is not enough to alleviate our anxiety. We may be suffering the pain of past traumas, buried emotional memories that go all the way back to childhood. While we may not consciously recall a particular traumatic incident or event, the memory — and the accompanying emotions — remain imprinted on our nervous system.

When a present situation arouses repressed childhood memories, we may not consciously think of the past event, but we reexperience the emotional pain. The result is often a chronic state of nameless anxiety, repeating fits of unexplained sadness or depression, or a state of burning anger and hostility toward life and the people we love.

Daily activities continually nudge our buried emotional pain back into consciousness because people and situations in our current lives often remind us of people and events from the past. This is no accident. We tend to seek out the familiar in our personal relationships.

This is one of the reasons men and women who grew up with an alcoholic parent often marry an alcoholic. If we were behaving logically, we would avoid associating with heavy drinkers or other drug users because we know from experience how much pain chemical dependency causes. But to us, chemical dependency seems "normal." It's what we're used to. We think we know how to deal with the cracker factory dynamics of dysfunctional relationships.

But put us in a healthy relationship and we're lost. If we grew up in a dysfunctional family, we've probably never learned how to cope with honesty, directness, caring, and consideration.

If we're still mired in addiction or codependency, we'll almost always pick a mate who operates on the same wavelength as we do. It's practically automatic.

Victor & Donna: Battered Adult Children

Victor, a recovering addict and codependent who grew up with a rejecting and abusive mother, explains it this way: "If you put me in a room with a hundred decent, honest, caring women and one witch, I will magnetically gravitate to the witch. I have an uncanny ability to pick out the one woman who will love me up and tear me down at the same time. If she's manipulative, needy, secretly hostile, and a little good-looking, I'll fall immediately in love. That's how my current wife, Donna, and I got together. We met at a party. She was drinking and crying in the corner, muttering about what jerks men were. She told me all about her alcoholic father and her drug addict ex-husband, and we ended up going home together. We got married a few months later."

Victor and Donna have been in a recovery program and

couples therapy for over a year, and they recognize that a lot of their problems stem from the traumas each experienced as children.

Victor says, "We're both working on changing ourselves because we want to be happy. But, my God, it's hard. I'm an intelligent person, but sometimes I feel like an emotional moron. Donna and I are both almost forty, but we're still battered children emotionally. We didn't start growing up until we got sober, and now we have a lot to learn about what it takes to be emotionally mature and happy people."

Donna thought her ever-present anxiety would disappear once she and her husband joined a recovery group. "Victor's been straight for over a year," she admits. "He's really doing well, working hard, bringing home a regular paycheck, the whole works. And I'm working my own program. I'm really trying to Let Go and Let God, but I don't know — I just can't relax. I feel like the roof is going to fall in any second. I make myself physically sick worrying."

Donna's experience is not unusual. Many recovering folks find it hard to let go of the past. Expectations of disaster are so ingrained that we may actually create problems, pick fights, and cause unnecessary trouble simply to relieve the tension of waiting.

Donna confesses, "Sometimes when things are going real smooth between Victor and me, I get real scared, like, you know, don't let yourself get too happy because someone'll come along and take it away. I feel so tense waiting around for doom to strike that my skin actually hurts. You know, like that old saying, feeling like you're going to jump out of your skin. Well, that's just what it's like. I can't stand it. It makes me crazy. So, what I'll do is, I'll pick a fight with Victor over some little thing. He says he doesn't understand why I can't let a good thing last, why I can't enjoy the good times. You see, it's like if I get too happy I might die or something. Or if I love Victor too much, the gods will see that I'm happy, and they'll reach right down and take him away from me. So if I rile things up a little it kind of relieves the tension of waiting for the gods to annihilate me. It's like, you know, if I start a fight it puts me in control and that way I don't feel so vulnerable and anxious."

Donna's insight is striking. A year ago she had no understanding or awareness of her behavior, no idea of why she was always picking fights. Therapy has helped her recognize the role her anxiety plays in the constant conflict in her relationships. Her next step is to confront her anxiety directly instead of avoiding it with diversion tactics.

Confronting her anxiety is painful for Donna because it means she has to confront not only her present behavior, but also the anger she's stockpiled for years against her alcoholic father.

It's no accident that Donna lives in dread of being struck down by an all-powerful being. She grew up with a capricious father, a man who charmed her and called her his Little Princess one moment, then reviled her and called her a slut the next. As a child she wanted nothing more nor less than her father's love and approval. And there were radiant moments of happiness when he smiled on her. But within days or hours, his drunken temper destroyed every shred of Donna's hope and happiness.

Most children view their parents as godlike creatures. Donna was no different. The tragedy of her life is that thirty years later she still expects the daddy-god to destroy her happiness.

For Donna, as for many of us, recovery means suffering through the anxiety that confronting her painful childhood involves. We can only let go of the past when we have the courage to stand up to it, saying, *You are over. You can no longer hurt me.*

Recovery from Resentment Wounds

Let's face it: Chemical dependency, whether we first encounter it as children or as adults, inflicts deep emotional wounds on addicts and on the people who love them.

When we begin the process of recovery, we're all hiding wounds that haven't been allowed to heal, *resentment wounds* — the gashes, traumas, and lacerations of the past. Our resentment wounds can damage our working relationships, destroy our marriages, and undermine our friendships. And, of course, resentment wounds can sabotage our recovery.

Living with chemical dependency is painful. Every member of the family lives with uncertainty, fear of emotional or physical abuse, and anxiety over their own well-being and for the safety of their loved ones. And they experience constant disappointment and anger over their feelings of powerlessness.

The pain we feel is real, the trauma is real, the anxiety is real. But there's nothing we can do to change the past. All we can change is the way we allow the past to affect us now. And we can't change the people who hurt us, either. The only person we have the power to change is ourselves. Luckily, when we change, the good effect often rubs off on the people closest to us.

ALL MEMBERS OF A CHEMICALLY DEPENDENT FAMILY SUFFER

Your pain is real, your anger is real and to be expected. But you can't change the past. You can only change yourself, today.

If, like Victor or Donna, we are suffering in the present because of past traumas, it is in our best interest to make every
effort to face our pain and fears directly. Yes, we may have
been deeply hurt in the past, but we are no longer the helpless,
frightened children of twenty, thirty, or forty years ago.

We are adults now, and as adults we have the capacity
to do whatever is necessary — including confronting our
most unspeakable fears — in order to heal the resentment
wounds of the past.

Recovery demands that we have the courage to change
what we can. Recovery also demands that, regardless of our
age, we accept the challenge of deciding who we are and
what we want to be when we grow up.

*Talented Screwballs: Their Own Worst Enemy**

"But I can't do anything about it!" — So goes the cry of a person chained to the past. But psychologist Albert Ellis contends that people have considerable control over their emotional distress. They cannot change the past, but they have the ability to stubbornly reject self-pity. Unfortunately, says Ellis, they often let self-pity get them down. Many persist in their distress and resist the best efforts of anyone who tries to help them.

Ellis, founder of the Institute of Rational Emotive Therapy in New York, calls these folks "talented screwballs."

Events and circumstances in the past and present don't make us unhappy, argues Ellis. What really disturbs us is our irrational beliefs about the past, or irrational beliefs about what's happening now. What are these beliefs?

- We *must* always do things perfectly.
- We always *have to* be perfect or outstanding in our achievements.
- We *should* live a long, happy, and enjoyable life.

Ellis has spent his professional life trying to dispel these "musts" and "shoulds." His clients are intelligent and well-motivated to change, but too often they remain stuck.

Ellis believes many of these "talented screwballs" fail in therapy because they set only short-term goals for their own gratification when long-term goals are in their best interest. A woman who fears elevators avoids them. A man who fears social rejection avoids new contacts. They see what they can do to make positive changes, but they do not make the changes. They also severely criticize themselves for failing — which increases their anxiety. Then they get depressed because they "can't do anything right."

What's the solution? *Understanding* the problem is just not enough. What works is to *take specific steps* to remedy the distress.

*Adapted from profile of Albert Ellis: "You Are What You Think," Claire Warga, Psychology Today, September 1988.

CHAPTER TWELVE

End Worry Now!

A Centipede was happy quite,
  Until a frog in fun
Said, "Pray, which leg comes after which?"
This raised her mind to such a pitch,
She lay distracted in the ditch
  Considering how to run.
                                —*Anonymous*

What? Me Worry?

Clyde worries, and he worries about his worrying. "I spend so much time worrying, I think I've got an internal worrywart, a built-in tape recorder that's always on, sending me small, panicky messages about the past and the future. I worry about what I did yesterday, and about what's going to happen tomorrow. If I ever get relaxed enough to turn my worrywart tape off, I worry that something's wrong because I'm simply not worrying like I usually do."

We may not worry as intensely as Clyde, but many of us are nattering nabobs of worry. We worry about money (not enough, bills, interest rates, credit). We agonize over relationships. (*Does he/she/it really like/love me?*) We worry about our performance. (*Will I make a fool out of myself? . . . Will I flub up again? . . . Will I pass? . . . Will I make the team? . . . Will they like me?*)

Our prayers seem to come out in a mangled form: *"Give us this day our daily dread."*

Worry is a common feature of many forms of anxiety. Psychologist Thomas D. Borkovec believes that worry is the cognitive component of anxiety. In other words, worry can be seen as a *mental symptom* of anxiety.

For most of us, says Borkovec, worry does not dominate our thoughts. When we worry, we think about ways to resolve problems or we mull over preparations for future events. Thoughts and images flow through our minds, but we can readily interrupt them. We may be preoccupied by our thoughts, but they do not cause us any added distress.

For some of us, however, worry seems to take on a life of its own. Troublesome thoughts and images flow relentlessly and distract from work and from enjoyment of leisure. Such worry does not produce any solutions. It is almost always tinged with negative emotions — especially fear and apprehension about the future. And because it seems to be uncontrollable, it increases emotional distress because most of us feel that it's important to be able to control our thoughts.

Worry may also intensify our anxiety. Worry usually involves a stream of negative and highly emotional thoughts and images. These emotionally charged thoughts and images can trigger physical reactions — raise blood pressure, increase heart rate, change breathing patterns, and so on. These changes, in turn, can distress us and cause us further anguish. Thus when we worry, we generate additional fear images and physical reactions, even in the absence of a real external threat.

Borkovec's studies of worry show that those who have uncontrollable thoughts and images are more anxious, depressed, angry, and self-conscious than non-worriers:

The greater amount of reported worry, the

more likely that the individual also will have fears of numerous objects and situations, particularly those involving social evaluations. [In one study] people worried most about fears of feeling self-conscious, making mistakes, meeting someone for the first time, failing tests, being criticized and being a leader.

Worry can also interfere with sleep. Uncontrollable intrusive thoughts and images at bedtime are a main cause of insomnia. Lack of sleep, of course, leads to increased irritability, anxiety, and other negative emotions.

The Controlled Fretting Exercise

What's the best way of breaking up the vicious circle of worry?

Borkovec suggests a self-control strategy based on learning theory. Since we can and do worry almost anywhere and anytime, our negative thoughts and images can readily become associated with many situations. To reduce the frequency of worry, Borkovec recommends that we try to limit the times and places where worry most commonly occurs. There are five rules for controlling worry:

1. Closely observe your thinking during the day and try to identify the times when worry begins and the places where you worry the most.

2. Each day, set aside a half-hour worry period — the same time, the same place every day.

3. Try to postpone your worrying until your worry period. When you catch yourself worrying outside your worry period, *STOP*. Remind yourself to worry later.

4. The best way to stop the intrusive thoughts and images is to focus attention *on something else*. Concentrate on the task at hand, or think about anything else in your immediate environment. This may be difficult to do at first, but keep at it. Like other forms of learning, this part takes practice. Above all, try to keep from worrying in bed. As an anonymous poet advised: "Don't wrestle your pillow, but lay down your head,/ And boot every worry right out of bed."

5. Use your daily worry period to worry. Don't dawdle and let your thoughts trip the light fantastic toe — get right down to the nitty gritty of *serious worry*. If you can't get started, you might prime the pump by thinking about the greenhouse effect, or about pesticides and herbicides in the food, or about the federal budget deficit, or about the homeless. (There's always the possibility that if you worry about these things, your own worries will seem a lot less troublesome.)

Real Problems Require Real Solutions

Most of our uncontrolled worry involves fear of criticism, fear of evaluation, fear of the future. But there's also a lot of worry about some very real problems. Money problems, house payments, relationships, jobs, and so on. While self-control strategies such as those suggested in the Controlled Fretting Exercise may help reduce the intensity of these worries and may somewhat lessen our anxiety, real problems require real solutions.

The basic problem is not worry — the basic problem is our own resistance to change.

We have two choices: (1) Do something about the source of our worry, or (2) keep on worrying. We may lessen the intensity of worry and anxiety by meditating, praying, relaxing, or drinking less coffee. But many times overcoming worry requires *problem-solving*. How do we get on top of worry?

Ask two questions:

1. *What is it — what, exactly, am I worried about?* Make a list of your most pressing concerns, your most nagging worries. Usually worries can be narrowed down to something fairly specific, like: *I'm worried about not having enough money to pay my bills.* (What bills? Utilities? Fuel? All bills? Be as specific as possible.) Or: *I'm worried that I might lose my job.* (Why? Is the plant shutting down? Are you having a conflict with your boss? Are you missing too much work?) Or: *I'm worried that my husband might leave me, and I'll have to take care of my kids by myself.* (Again, be specific.)

Sometimes worry seems so vague that it doesn't seem to be *about* anything. "I'm worried about *everything*." Well, that may be, but if we try to do *something* about *everything*, we usually end up doing *nothing* at all.

2. *What can I do about it?* This is where many of us come to a dead standstill. We can identify our chief worry, but we seem to be helpless to do anything about it. We get stuck in a worry cycle: Worry makes us feel helpless. And then feelings of helplessness cause us to worry even more.

Here are some other places where we often get stuck in a worry cycle:

- "I have so many bills, I'll *never* get out of debt."

- "My supervisor doesn't like me, and I know she's out to get me. It's all office politics — I can't do anything to stop it."
- "I just know we're headed for a divorce, and I feel so helpless. I can't even talk about it. If I went to get help, my husband would get so mad he'd leave me for sure."

How do we get out of a worry cycle? By looking at our worry as a *problem with a solution.*

REMINDER

We can always do *something* about worry.

"Yeah!" Or "Yeah, But"?

This is where *attitude* is of paramount importance. We can approach worry with a defeatist, close-minded attitude (*I'm helpless. I can't do anything about it*), in which case we will get stuck in the worry cycle.

Or we can approach worry with an open mind, honestly looking at our resources, talents, and abilities.

Too often we give up too soon without making an honest effort to consider what we might be able to do. We discount possible solutions by coming up with excuses that start: "Yeah, but . . . "

So if we decide that we really want to do something about our worry, we must then decide on a course of action. Every worry has one or more possible solutions, and some solutions might be more effective than others.

Bills? Cut up credit cards. (*Yeah!*) Get help from a consumer credit counselor. (*Yeah!*) Spend 25 percent of every paycheck on lottery tickets. (*Boo!*) Borrow money from a loan shark. (*Boo!*) Go to Atlantic City or Las Vegas to hit it big at blackjack or the slots or roulette. (*Boo!*)

Addicted spouse? Seek help — from an addictions counselor, Al-Anon, or a family-oriented treatment program. (*Yeah!*) Pretend the problem doesn't exist. (*Boo!*) Nag, but don't seek help yourself. (*Boo!*) Complain to family members or friends, but refuse to talk to a specialist in family intervention. (*Boo!*)

Insecure about a relationship? Change your attitude and behaviors. (*Yeah!*) Go to a counselor alone if your partner won't cooperate. (*Yeah!*) Try to change partner without looking at your own behavior. (*Boo!*) Stay a victim. (*Boo!*) Stick your head in the sand, worrying, complaining, and hoping for your partner to become transformed into the person you want. (*Boo!*)

Where Do We Go Wrong?

- *We try to change the things we cannot change and ignore the things we can change.* We may try to change the way another person acts, feels, or thinks, while we ignore the changes we can make in our own thoughts, feelings, attitudes, and behavior.

"But it's not my fault — why should I have to be the one to do everything? I'm the victim." True, our creditors may harass and threaten us unmercifully. Our partner may be thoughtless, inconsiderate, and hypercritical. Our supervisor may be totally unreasonable and unfair — but we do not have the power to make others behave the way we'd like them to behave. We *do* have the power to change the way we behave.

- *We seek a* **permanent solution** *for all our worries.* We'd like a nice, tidy, simple, lasting solution. We don't just want to find some way of dealing with specific worries — we want to vanquish distress from our lives like a super-strength detergent removes ring-around-the-collar.

But there's no permanent solution for all worry because, like anxiety, we can't totally escape from worry. What we can do, however, is make our worry manageable. We can learn to take worry in stride, place it in a proper perspective, and get on with our lives.

- *We want someone else to do it*. We can identify our worry, but we want someone else to take charge and make our lives worry-free.
- *We don't consider a solution to be possible unless it is painless, easy, and effortless*. We want to win the lottery so we can pay all our bills and not have to worry about money anymore. (And we overlook the fact that sudden money brings its own set of burdens and worries.) We want our supervisor to look past our performance into our soul, to see the real, worthy person inside. We want to have total security in a relationship, and we want to depend on our spouse to provide all.

What goes wrong is this: We believe there are fast solutions to troubles, but we just haven't been able to find the right combination. And we are creatures of habit who find it more comfortable to hold on to present worries and anxieties than to take steps to lessen our worries. Change always involves uncertainty (which makes us even more anxious and worried). And there is no guarantee of success.

Alvin Toffler described this kind of passive resistance to change, in his book, *Future Shock*. Change always involves psychological costs, says Toffler — time and effort and new adaptive responses: "In a familiar context, we are able to handle many of our life problems with low-cost programmed [habitual] decisions. Change and novelty boost the psychic price of decision-making. When we move to a new neighborhood, for example, we are forced to alter old relationships and establish new routines or habits."

This can't be done without first discarding thousands of old habits and routines and beginning the task of learning new relationships, habits, and routines. It's a psychologically costly form of reprogramming our lives.

So we stick with our old, familiar worry cycle because it troubles us even less than the prospect of action and change. And because our solutions may not be perfect ones.

Avoiding the Pitfalls of Perfectionism

> *Lord, grant me the serenity*
> *To do what I can do,*
> *To give it my best shot*
> *And to be reasonably satisfied*
> *If it doesn't come out perfect.*
> *— Recovering Perfectionist's Prayer*

If you are a perfectionist, you are bound to be a loser at whatever you do. A consummate failure. A sublime flop.

A perfectionist will always fail to meet the elevated standards of perfection. If examined with a critical eye, everything, every person, every idea falls short of perfection. Only in the movies was Bo Derek a "10." And even there, the critics ranked her acting "3" or below.

Likewise, every achievement falls short of perfection. It can be fixed up, honed, modified, fine-tuned, and tinkered with in some way to make it "better."

When we pursue perfection, we will inevitably run headlong into frustration, worry, and self-hate.

Our perfectionistic tendency is usually so ingrained that

it has become an unthinking emotional reflex for us. Breaking our reflexive responses takes both effort and practice.

And patience.

Anti-Perfection Exercise:
Doing It Right (No Bad Dogs)

Perfectionists are world-class experts at negative self-talk. We go around saying the equivalent of "bad dog!" to ourselves all day. Then we lay in bed at night going over everything we did wrong today.

We know how to focus with exquisite precision on our shortcomings. We catalog every mistake, blunder, and clumsy encounter. *Why did I say this? . . . Why didn't I say that? . . . Did they like me? . . . Why did they give me that funny look? Jeez, I must have been a bad dog again. . . .* And on and on.

We fall asleep counting shortcomings instead of sheep. No wonder we feel anxious.

Thought Stopping for Perfectionists

Tonight, try something different. When your mind starts racing with negativity, and you hear yourself going into your Bad Dog Routine, say to yourself, *NO! Not now. I'm not going to dwell on the negative.*

This is a technique called *thought stopping,* and it works.

After you have ordered yourself to stop the negative self-talk, substitute at least five minutes of positive self-talk. What did you do right today? How many things can you count that are positive? Pay special attention to the little things you just normally expect of yourself.

Jeez, pardner, I tried it, but I just couldn't think of a durn gol-danged thang I did right today!

So it goes.

Our perfectionistic negativity may be so automatic, so ingrained and habitual, we can't think of a single thing we did right. But we usually do a lot of good things we take for granted — like getting to work on time, passing up that second piece of chocolate cake, making a dreaded phone call, being patient with a rude store clerk, and so on. We don't need to score big — just to appreciate all the good, ordinary, normal things we accomplish in a day.

ON THE OTHER HAND, WE MAY BE BAD DOGS.

All kidding aside, and tongue totally out of cheek, the purpose of this exercise is to break the emotional reflex of negative self-appraisal. If negativity creeps in, say *NO! Not now!* and continue giving yourself positive feedback.

Practice Makes Imperfect

This doesn't mean that we should never again critique our behavior for areas that need improvement. We all need to do that occasionally. But we perfectionists get carried away with the habit. What we really need is *balance*. And we need to practice patting ourselves on the back for all the things we usually take for granted.

This exercise will be most effective if we practice it at least five minutes a night over a period of weeks. It takes time to replace the habit of negative self-appraisal with the habit of positive self-appraisal.

Remember this point well, because our perfectionistic reflex will make us want to become flawless experts in positive self-talk in just one night.

Righting Real Wrongs

A final note on worry: *We may be worried sick about real wrongs.*

What real wrongs? Usually these kinds of worry involve violations of our higher values. We cheat on our spouse. We pilfer stamps, small change, or office supplies from our employer. We lie. We finagle our taxes.

And we're worried that we may be found out.

These worries are solid, grounded in what we know about ourselves and our values. And they are also grounded in our knowledge of real consequences.

We could get fired for pilfering. A frivolous one-nighter could end in a vicious, cutthroat divorce.

These kinds of real worries won't go away by thought-stopping or controlled fretting. They may plague us until we go into a tailspin of depression and anxiety.

Again, the two-step problem-solving technique outlined on page 127 will help with these worries. Be quite certain you know exactly what your real worry is.

And then stop doing whatever generates worry.

This sounds simple, and it is. But oddly, we often don't want to stop doing the very thing that worries us. We don't want to do the obvious — stop the troublesome and distressing behavior. We want to be able to continue the behavior worry-free. We want to find excuses for behaving badly. We try to find reasons why it's okay to steal from our employer. (*He doesn't pay me what I'm worth.*) We rationalize our sordid affairs. (*What he/she doesn't know won't hurt him/her.*) We find extenuating circumstances. (*Everybody cheats on their taxes.*)

We can't have it both ways.

The most effective solution for the kind of worry that comes from a violation of our higher values is this: Stop the behavior now. And make amends if possible.

*Transcendental Metaworry**

Worry, says biology watcher Dr. Lewis Thomas, is the most spontaneous and natural of human functions. With tongue in cheek, Dr. Thomas argues that worry is a gift that distinguishes humans from other forms of life. "Man," says Dr. Thomas, "is the Worrying Animal."

Worry certainly didn't originate in the twentieth century. Worry didn't originate with technological complexity. Dr. Thomas suggests that prehistoric man may have been the most anxious of us all. "Fumbling about in dimly lit caves, trying to figure out what he ought really to be doing, sensing the awesome responsibilities for toolmaking just ahead, he must have spent a lot of time contemplating his thumbs and fretting about them. I can imagine him staring at his hands, apposing thumbtips to each fingertip in amazement, thinking, By God, that's something to set us apart from the animals — and then the grinding thought, What on earth are they for? There must have been many long sleepless nights, his mind all thumbs."

The problem is, we don't do it well enough. Our worry awaits perfection. Dr. Thomas proposes a technique called *Transcendental Worry* — best practiced in twenty-minute sessions of purposeful muscular tension, discomfort, and breathing through one nostril at a time, alternating sides with each breath. Rapidly repeat the word *worry* and after about three minutes you will become aware of concentrated, irreversible trouble. You see that continental drift is unpreventable and that moon gravity causes baldness. When thoughts like these begin to occur, you have entered the highest stage — pure worry about pure worry. This, says Dr. Thomas, is the essence of the Wisdom of the West.

He calls it *Transcendental Metaworry.*

* Adapted from *The Medusa and the Snail: More Notes of a Biology Watcher*, Lewis Thomas, New York: Viking, 1979.

CHAPTER THIRTEEN

Embracing Life: The Wisdom of Buddha & Satchel Paige

During active addiction and codependency we live a lifestyle that embraces self-destruction. We are committing slow suicide, living lives of despair and pain.

When we choose recovery, we are turning away from self-annihilation. But turning away from death is not the same thing as embracing life.

— *If* we continue abusing our bodies . . .
— *If* we spend our time in darkened rooms smoking cigarettes and swilling coffee . . .
— *If* we let anxiety eat away at our innards and do little to change ourselves because we refuse to engage fully in the *recovery effort* . . .
— *If* we avoid the legitimate suffering that comes with positive change . . .

. . . Then we are still living a marginal sort of existence, a marginal recovery, even if we call ourselves recovering.

Emotional well-being is only possible when we reject self-destruction and embrace life wholeheartedly.

This means rejecting the old bad habits of excess. It means working our programs of recovery until it becomes habitual. And it means caring enough to live clean and healthy lives.

This will be hard for us at first because old (bad) habits die hard. This will be hard because, as Albert Ellis indicates, many of us are talented screwballs who seem determined to avoid the things we can change.

But the payoff is worth it. *You are worth it.*

The Inner Music — A Fable for Recovering Folks

Long ago in a faraway kingdom, a young prince named Shona dedicated himself to the teachings of Buddha. When Buddha was visiting the capital, the Prince heard him speak and was deeply moved. He immediately renounced his kingdom and all its luxuries, and he asked to be initiated as a sannyasin [apprentice monk].

Buddha did not want the Prince to act so impulsively. "Wait," Buddha said. "I'll be here for four months. Think and study. Then you can be initiated."

"No," the young man replied. "The decision has happened; there is nothing more to think about. Why are you telling me to wait four months? I don't want to wait a single day."

Buddha, moved by the Prince's passion and sincerity, relented, allowing Shona to be initiated. Still, Buddha had misgivings. The life of the initiate was difficult. It was a great arduous phenomenon, one Buddha had experienced himself. But Buddha had taken his time. It had taken him six years to become enlightened.

Slowly, slowly Buddha had become accustomed to the difficult life, a contemplative life without luxuries. He marveled when people ridiculed and reviled him for no good reason, for he wasn't hurting anyone.

He came to see that people who are confused and bewildered lack understanding and vision.

In their confusion, they mistake numbness, apathy, and self-preoccupation for peace and serenity.

They mistake intoxication for the ferment of inner joy.

They mistake tinsel and bauble and gaud for the splendor of life.

They live such lies that whenever they see a person of truth they are wounded of their own accord — they feel hurt, insulted.

But Shona surprised Buddha. The ex-prince did not strain against his arduous new life. He went to the extreme. Other monks ate but once a day; the new monk, the former hedonist, ate only once every two days. Other monks slept under trees; Shona slept in open fields. The other monks walked barefoot on the open roads; he walked barefoot beside the roads, stepping on stones and thorns.

Other monks came to Buddha and said, "Something has to be done. That man has gone to the extreme. He doesn't understand the true meaning of our life. He is showing off and it is making him ill."

One night Buddha went to the ex-prince and said, "Shona, may I ask you a question?"

Shona replied, "Of course, my Lord. I am your disciple."

Buddha said, "I have heard that when you were a prince you were a great musician; you used to play the sitar."

Shona said, "Yes, I used to practice eight hours a day, and I had become famous all over the country. But that is all finished now."

Buddha said, "I have to ask one question. If the strings of your sitar are too tight, what will happen?"

Shona replied, "It is simple. The strings will be broken. You cannot play upon them."

Buddha said, "Another question: What will happen if they are too loose?"

Shona replied, "That too is simple. If they are too loose they will produce no music — there will be no tension."

Buddha said, "You are an intelligent person — I need not say more. Remember, life is also a musical instrument. It needs a certain tension, but only a certain tension. If your life is too loose, there is no music. But if it is too tight, you start breaking down — again there is no music. Remember it. First, you lived a very loose life and you missed the inner music. Now, you are living a very tight life and you are still missing the music. Is there not a way to adjust the strings of the sitar right in the middle, so they are neither too tight nor too loose, so there is just the right amount of tension and the music can arise?"

"Yes," Shona replied. "With proper study a musician can learn just the proper tension."

Buddha said, "That is my teaching to you: Be exactly in the middle between the two poles. The tension does not have to disappear completely — without tension there is no music. But the tension should not become too much, because you will break and, again, you will make no music. Either extreme and your life is madness."

The Wisdom of Leroy Satchel Paige

Once in a land far away in the kingdom of the major leagues, there was a prince of a baseball player named Leroy Satchel Paige. No one knew how old he was, but there were stories that it was Satchel Paige who taught old Abner Doubleday all he knew about the game of "beisboll" in Cooperstown, New York, one lazy summer afternoon in 1839.

There are others who say this is myth, stuff and nonsense — the diaphanous fabric that dreams and poetry and base-ball magic are made of.

This much, however, is true:

Leroy Satchel Paige mastered the game of baseball and played for twenty-five years before blacks were allowed in the major leagues. He was perhaps the best pitcher of his era. He pitched three thousand games and sent opposing teams scoreless and humiliated to the locker room three hundred times. In addition to these shutouts, he pitched an unprecedented fifty no-hitters.

In 1948, forty-two-year-old Satchel Paige was the first black major league pitcher, and when he hurled the legendary horsehide, they say at times it traveled faster than a speeding bullet — or the ball would dip and slide past baffled batters — as if in another uncanny dimension, under the total control of the canny master of the game.

Satchel Paige stayed active in Major League Baseball far beyond the age that most ball-players hang up their mitts and retire. When he pitched for Kansas City in 1965, he was the oldest person to appear in a major league game. He was fifty-nine and still going strong.

Leroy Satchel Paige was known for his grace under pressure — for his ability to remain calm and get the swamp drained when he was up to his elbows in alligators.

He attributed his staying power and his success to six rules of living — his own unique recipe for staying free from worry and anxiety, alert, and life-affirming:

Satchel Paige's Rules for Living

- Avoid fried foods which angry up the blood.
- If your stomach disputes you, lie down and pacify it with cooling thoughts.
- Keep the juice flowing by jangling around gently as you go.
- Go very lightly on the vices such as carrying on in society — the social ramble ain't restful.
- Avoid running at all times.
- Don't look back. Somethin' might be gaining on you.

Notes & References

Page

Chapter One

5-6   *The Road Less Traveled*, M. Scott Peck, M.D., New York: Simon & Schuster (Touchstone Books), 1978, 16-17.

Chapter Two

20   Power of small, strong choices: Adapted from *Strong Choices, Weak Choices: The Challenge of Change in Recovery*, Gayle Rosellini and Mark Worden, Center City, Minn.: Hazelden Educational Materials, 1988.

Chapter Three

26   Adapted from *Taming Your Turbulent Past*, Gayle Rosellini and Mark Worden, Pompano Beach, Fla.: Health Communications, 1987.

31   Abstinence phobia, see: "The Abstinence Phobias: Links Between Substance Abuse and Anxiety," Sharon M. Hall, in *The International Journal of the Addictions*, 19:6, 1984, 613-31.

Chapter Four

37   Craving: "The Mystery of Craving," Arnold M. Ludwig, M.D., *Alcohol Health and Research World*, Fall 1986, 14-15.

Chapter Five

43   For estimates of anxiety disorders in addicts, see "The Prevalence of Psychiatric Disorders in Patients with Alcohol and Drug Problems," Helen E. Ross, Ph.D., Frederick B. Glaser, M.D., and Teresa Germanson, Sc.D., *Archives of General Psychiatry*, 45: 1023-31, 1988.

49   Canadian study: Ibid.

51   Hyperventilation: Adapted from "Hyperventilation, Anxiety, Craving for Alcohol: A Subacute Alcohol Withdrawal Syndrome," Sarah M. Roelofs, *Alcohol*, 1985, 2: 501-5; and "Hyperventilation and Anxiety: Alcohol Withdrawal Symptoms Decreasing with Prolonged Abstinence," Sarah M. Roelofs and Gerard M. Dikkenberg, *Alcohol*, 1987, 4:215-20.

Chapter Seven

66   AA position on medication: *The A.A. Member — Medications and Other Drugs*, New York: Alcoholics Anonymous World Services, Inc., 1984, 9.

68   Shut up and take your Valium: *I Want to Change, But I Don't Know How!* Tom Rusk, M.D. and Randy Read, M.D., Los Angeles: Price/Stern/Sloane, 1980, 249-50.

69   Pills and perfection: *There's Gold in Them Thar Pills: An Inquiry into the Medical-Industrial Complex*, Alan Klass, Baltimore: Penguin Books, 1975, 43.

70   *The Tranquilizing of America: Pill Popping and the American Way of Life*, Richard Hughes and Robert Brewin, New York: Harcourt Brace Jovanovich, 1979, 15.

73   Rush to medication: From *Mood Control*, Gene Bylinsky, New York: Scribners, 1978, 157.

Part Three

75   *The Search for Serenity: Understanding and Overcoming Anxiety*, Daniel A. Sugarman, Ph.D. and Lucy Freeman, New York: Macmillan, 1970, vii.

Chapter Eight

80   Huxley quote: *Aldous Huxley: A Biography*, Sybille Bedford, New York: Alfred A. Knopf and Harper & Row, 1973, 1974, 656.

83   Misdiagnosis: See *The Good News About Panic, Anxiety & Phobias*, Mark Gold, New York: Villard Books, 1989, 99-105.

84   Drug-Induced anxiety: From Alan Lipschitz, "Diagnosis and Classification of Anxiety Disorders," in *Handbook of Anxiety Disorders*, edited by Cynthia G. Last and Michel Herson, New York: Pergamon Press, 1988, 53.

85   Caffeinism: "Psychophysiological Aspects of Caffeine Consumption," John B. Murray, *Psychological Reports*, 62:575-87, 1988. For Greden quote, see Mark Worden and Gayle Rosellini, "Role of Diet in People-Work: Uses of Nutrition in Therapy with Substance Abusers," *Journal of Orthomolecular Psychiatry*, 7:4, 1978, 249-57. See also *The Good News About Panic, Anxiety & Phobias*, Mark Gold, New York: Villard Books, 1989, 138.

Chapter Nine

96   *Beyond the Relaxation Response*, Herbert Benson, New York: Times Books, 1984. See also *Your Maximum Mind*, Herbert Benson and William Proctor, New York: Times Books, 1987.

99   Skilled meditator in the looney bin: From *High Level Wellness: An Alternative to Doctors, Drugs, and Diseases*, Donald B. Ardell, Emmaus, Pa.: Rodale Press, 1977, 143. The second edition is available from Ten Speed Press.

102   Fitness and recovery: Patricia A. Murray, "Fitness and Recovery," *Alcohol Health and Research World*, Fall 1986, 30. See also J. Palmer, N. Vacc, and J. Epstein, "Adult Inpatient Alcoholics: Physical Exercise as a Treatment Intervention," *Journal of Studies on Alcohol*, 47:5, 418-21, 1988.

Chapter Ten

103   Quote by Stewart Emery: *Actualizations: You Don't Have to Rehearse to Be Yourself*, Stewart Emery, New York: Doubleday, 1978, 76-77.

109   Norman Jolliffe on sugar: "Alcohol and Nutrition: The Diseases of Chronic Alcoholism," Norman Jolliffe, *Alcohol, Science, and Society*, New Haven, Conn.: Quarterly Journal of Studies on Alcohol, 1945.

111   Caffeine and PMS: See "Premenstrual Syndrome: The Caffeine Connection," *Psychology Today*, June 1989, 13. See also "Tea and Premenstrual Syndrome in the People's Republic of China," Annette McKay Rossignol, Sc.D., Jianyi Zhang, M.D., Yongzhou Chen, M.D., and Zhen Xiang, M.D., *American Journal of Public Health*, 79:1, January 1989; and "Caffeine-containing Beverages and Premenstrual Syndrome in Young Women," Annette McKay Rossignol, *American Journal of Public Health*, 75:11, November 1985.

Chapter Eleven

121   "Talented Screwballs": Adapted from profile of Albert

Ellis: "You Are What You Think," Claire Warga, *Psychology Today*, 22:9, September 1988.

Chapter Twelve

123   Distracted Caterpillar poem: Anonymous, in *An Anthology of Light Verse*, edited by Louis Kronenberger, New York: Random House (Modern Library), 1935, 161. Suggestions for overcoming worry can be found in Dale Carnegie's book, *How to Stop Worrying and Start Living*, New York: Simon & Schuster (Pocket Books), 1948.

124   Borkovec's studies: Thomas D. Borkovec, "What's the Use of Worrying?" *Psychology Today*, December 1985, 59-64. See also "Stimulus Control Applications to the Treatment of Worry," T. D. Borkovec, Lenore Wilikinson, Roland Folensbee, and Caryn Lerman, *Behavior Research and Therapy*, 21:3, 247-51, 1983; "Preliminary Exploration of Worry: Some Characteristics and Processes," T. D. Borkovec, Elwood Robinson, Thomas Pruzinsky, and James A. DePree, *Behavior Research and Therapy*, 21:1, 9-16, 1981.

130   Toffler quote: *Future Shock*, Alvin Toffler, New York: Bantam Books, 1971, 357.

135   Lewis Thomas on Transcendental Metaworry: From *The Medusa and the Snail: More Notes of a Biology Watcher*, Lewis Thomas, New York: Viking, 1979, 82-87.

Chapter Thirteen

140   The Wisdom of Satchel Paige: The information about Satchel Paige and his rules of living are adapted from *The People's Almanac*, David Wallechinsky and Irving Wallace, Garden City, New York: Doubleday, Inc., 1975, 1062.